Exit Stage Left

TILLY DUNN

ISBN 978-1-957582-78-8 (paperback)
ISBN 978-1-957582-79-5 (hardcover)
ISBN 978-1-957582-77-1 (eBook)

Printed in the United States of America

WESTPOINT
PRINT AND MEDIA

CONTENTS

ENDORSEMENTS

What a good read!

What an incredible journey this book takes you through. I could almost feel the pain that would be brought about by these manic episodes, and I have a deep felt respect that she was able to pull out of it. Talk about determination and the Power of the mind and will! I also have lots of respect for Rob in sticking by Tilly through it all. It's certainly not easy to be with someone who is diagnosed bipolar or Borderline Personality Disorder, and in most cases, the relationship doesn't survive. BPD is further explained in other books such as "Stop Walking on Eggshells", that will help you understand what it's all about, and to appreciate even more what Tilly endured all of these years. Coming from myself, who holds a PhD in Applied Sciences, I am quite familiar with chemical imbalances, and I can surely understand and appreciate the pain she endured, and how those around her could feel helpless in these moments of trouble.

The book takes you through the years leading up to today, which I think is crucial to understanding that there was no real reason for the manic moments. Like Tilly, you must want the change badly enough to make the necessary steps towards it. I found this book to be an incredibly good read, and I would highly recommend it: either as a foundation to help in overcoming the condition, or to broaden your knowledge through someone else's eyes. Thank you, Tilly, for painstakingly telling us your story, and I know you'll stay true to your path.

Don Boulay, Ph.D., MBA, MCP.

Exit stage Left is the story of triumph over years of depression, anxiety and manic behavior: not one dark night of the soul, but many. Tilly's grit and determination to learn, grow and finally to change her path is inspirational. Her story reads like fiction, but it is her truth. I was honored to be part of her journey and I am so proud that she is now opening up and sharing with others. Her light is a beacon to those in pain. Her book isn't simply, how she did it. It's much more. It's how you can make gentle change daily and move from your darkness into your light.

Jacqueline Fairbrass R R Pr
Dynamic Compassion Mentoring
Feeling Absolutely Fabulous Llc
Founder, School of Complementary Therapies

"Authentic, real, and raw! Exit Stage Left is as unique as the author who wrote it. Tilly Dunn gently and sincerely opens her heart to share with you from her deepest sorrows to her greatest blessings. As you read this book, allow yourself to be inspired by the enormous possibilities and opportunities available to you to move forward with a joyful spirit."

Peggy McColl, New York Times bestselling author

"Exit Stage Left guides us to the light in our own darkness and shows us how determination and a new focus on gratitude and generosity can change your life for the better, one emotion at a time. Love is always the answer."

Tracy Friesen, author of Ride the Waves Volumes I & II

"What an amazing story of courage and inspiration. Exit Stage Left is a fascinating journey, an eye opener…on a topic we know so little about. Most of us have only scratched the surface, but Tilly Dunn takes you on a deep dive as she shares her experience with mental turmoil and depression. Get ready to be shaken yet equipped to celebrate life with the author as she delivers a real-life account of pain and suffering and how she now celebrates life to the maximum."

Rodney Flowers, bestselling author of Get Up!
I Can't. I Will. I Did…Here's How!

Dear Reader

This book is for you who wants a greater understanding into the mind of a suicidal person, or also, into the mind of someone who has been diagnosed psychotic. It is my story, published for the third time. The first edition referred to my sister without printing her name. The second edition, although this had my sister's name published in it, was with a discontinued publisher. And, so here is the third edition. My altruistic reason for wanting my own success is because a greater understanding of why these thoughts exist is sorely needed. My toes, dipped into the water with the first book, had me survive well. ESL was flagged as a worthwhile book to read. Please benefit from my experience because knowledge is power. Truly, history does not have to repeat itself.

We have learned that affirmations, attitudes of gratitude, and manifestations are now our reality. Let's move on to better mental health care using lessons learned. Rob and I celebrated 50 years of marriage in 2018, and both of us have noticed that the information technology has gathered steam. Knowledge is exponentially accelerating and personally, I would like this to translate into a coming Heaven on Earth, otherwise known as Utopia; inclusive in its' nature.

I will describe in greater detail what my thinking patterns are in my next book, Enter Stage Right. My inability to cope with my mental pain brought on suicidal ideation for 51 years. Then, Laser surgery that released my pinched spinal cord at L5S1 in Nov. 2007 had the unexpected bonus of relieving me of my suicidal thoughts. I cannot explain the connection between my back surgery and suicidal thinking relief.

Our world is in such flux that mentors encourage you to be flexible. You never know what tomorrow brings. Live and enjoy the moment.

My first book is called "Exit Stage Left", or "ESL". These three letters also mean English as a Second Language and I secretly chuckled at their doubled meaning. In this book, I describe in detail my four parents who gave me my foundation in my first six years of life. Truthfully, only two of these four parents were on my radar. They were called Tante Jannie and Oom Cees, or T.J. and O.C. These words would equate as Mother and Father to me, or Mom and Dad to most of you. I was their only child, and my nickname was 'TIP'.

This was a simple name for me and life was all about simplicity. My life was full of feeling, and that feeling consisted mainly of a "sense of abundance". Without repeating this "sense", know that it existed in all that I describe during our years together. The love that flowed between Tante Jannie, Oom Cees and myself, was in the air. Each day was so precious: to be met with joyous anticipation. We lived in a little house in the woods that I just loved. The woods all around the house were an extension of our abode. At first, there was no electricity and no telephone. But while in my toddler years, our hand pump moved from outside our front door to inside. The red indoor hand pump, which I saw as a luxury, brought our lives into the glorious pleasure of having water come from indoors. We also had an indoor outhouse, which when I think back on it, did not smell. The W.C. (water closet) was a small square room that across one wall had a shiny lacquered wooden bench, which contained a "bum sized" hole with a well-fitted wooden lid on it. These were the years from 1945 to 1951; my first six years. I'm describing what was important to me in those first years.

There are more stories that give you a view from the inside. My passion for sharing with you my experiences are hopefully going to translate into treating those who are mentally struggling, with a greater understanding and compassion.

We all meet people along the way who improve our lives. Make the best of what you have been given. Go towards those who inspire you, uplift you and empower you. I am full of feeling and just like you, I am allowed to be who I am. Hold love and forgiveness in your heart like I do. Over the years, my love and forgiveness have grown to proportions I never thought possible. It keeps growing expansively. Enjoy!

Love,

Xoxox
Tilly

CHAPTER 1

Early Duality

People often think that when you're depressed, you've been that way for your entire life. But that's not often the case. At least, it wasn't the case for me. Not until after I turned six, was depression a feeling, a condition that grew inside. It started like a small seed of doubt, an uncomfortable inner thought, and quickly grew, spiraling out of control. It was agitated and increased by my life's events. For me, depression was something that was turned on like a light switch. It was the loss of my godparents at the age of six, which turned on the switch. I had a trauma at the age of six that I didn't recover from. I believe now that I had PTSD (Post Traumatic Stress Disorder) at this age. That's a big claim for me to make and, when I read the symptoms, I had them. Read my story and decide for yourself. It was a disorder that I struggled and dealt with on my own during most of my life. Sure, there were plenty of events and experiences that magnified and nurtured its growth, but that growth was more like a tumor and less like a flower.

Depression grew inside me until it began to suffocate me. My heart and soul were overtaken and felt cloudier by the day. This is the story of my journey. This is the story of my decline and eventual landing at rock bottom, and then remaining there for quite a long time. But thankfully that's only a small part of my journey. It's not where it ended but rather it's where it began. My climb and ascent from rock bottom to a life capable of finding and embracing happiness wasn't easy, but I did it. And if I can do it, so can others burdened with mental disorders.

The February 2015 issue of "NATIONAL GEOGRAPHIC" has an article called "The Invisible War on the Brain". As the years rolled by for me, I battled silently by myself against what I was experiencing with my own mind. This article is a big piece of the puzzle, in my view. You will read in Chapter 1 that my mother was carrying me near the stairs when a piece of shrapnel came through a thick oak door with such force that my father, a surgeon, had to remove this piece through the other side of her big calf. The article writes of the variety of symptoms that might occur and I relate so very much to these. I hypothesize that my delayed speech was not only due to "The Hunger Winter" but also to the exposure of the close blast as a newborn baby.

Even through years of counseling or assessment visits, I wasn't given the occasion or the encouragement to go into detail on my first six years of life. This opportunity to write the story of my life is a gift. For whatever reason, no one thought that those first years played a role in where I am today. But I am confident that if you look towards the first six years of your life, it may help you to understand where and who you are today. We are encouraged these days to look forward and not back. A good time to look back, though, is when we are actively working at why it is so difficult to pull out of a rut.

There was an early duality for me. At first I thought I had one mother and one father. These I called Tante Jannie and Oom Cees. *Tante* means aunt in Dutch and *Oom* means uncle. They are T.J. and O.C. and I refer to them as my godparents. I was not aware of the actual difference between aunt and uncle and mother and father. But when I was five years old, I became aware that I really "belonged" to two families. And one family was very different from the other. Actually the duality was not confusing to me while I was growing and learning the basics of life because my life was full of love and simplicity. It's well known that little children are resilient in the circumstances in which they find themselves. But the emigration from Holland to Canada left me with a feeling of shock and then discomfort. This feeling was never addressed and lived inside me until well after my teenage years.

Biologically, I came from a large nuclear family of eight. My parents and five older brothers and sisters lived in the city Apeldoorn, The Netherlands. But my godparents and I lived in the country, just a few miles out of town, in the woods. The dynamics of each of these families was completely different and with reading my story, you'll discover how. Look for the relation to your own circumstances. This is how my story may help you.

My mother and my godmother loved me. My father and my godfather loved me. My brothers and sisters treated me like their baby sister, which I was. Our family dynamic seemed normal at the time, but in hindsight, it was quite unique. I simply never understood the divide. It left me filled with many questions and constantly looking for an unobtainable identity and clarity.

So I became a person who tried to deal with my questions on my own. At an early age I kept my thoughts to myself. That continued over time. In the summer of 1951, when I was six, my city family immigrated to Canada; and I went with them. To that point, my life felt balanced and I was a happy young girl because I was showered with the exclusive love and care of Tante Jannie, Oom Cees and their entire extended families. I was T.J and O.C's "only child". In later years I learned that they were unable to have children biologically, thus I was blessed and loved beyond description.

But depression hit me hard when we arrived at our destination in Canada. I felt abandoned by my psychological "parents" with their large extended family, even though I knew that they were not responsible for my circumstances. They were all living in Holland and I was desperate to be with them. On the boat to Canada I was in deep shock and today I still have no memories of the voyage. I no longer need them to move forward with my healthy mind. My first years in Canada were a blur. Even so, I became hyper-vigilant.

While in Holland, I felt loved and supported and actually enjoyed having two families in two homes. My greatest comfort level and sense of belonging was with Tante Jannie and Oom Cees. When my "new" family arrived at our destination in Canada, my reality hit me. I had not been confiding in any of these family members whom I had never really gotten to know. I felt lost and abandoned, even though I was with my "real" family.

It was that loss that plunged me into a deep depression. How could this be? Why was I so sad? I was supposed to be a little "sunshine" everywhere I went. These were the silent questions that I asked myself when I realized that I wasn't coping well after the move. I denied the depression to myself for years. When I was a child, it wasn't recognized that children could suffer from depression. Not only is it clear now that I was depressed, but it developed into something more serious and long-standing.

My Four Parents

My biological mother and father were both born in 1906. They were children during the first World war. They met when they were both in high school and my father asked my mother to marry him when they were 18. Theirs was a long engagement because they didn't get married until July, 1931. My father was all set to become an astronomer, his first love, but His sense of duty prevailed. Hitler was a Right-Wing Fascist and he had a charisma that was frightening for anyone who did not fall for his fear tactics.

In fact, my mother was so angry at the rising social climate that she sewed a big yellow star on the jackets of her school aged children. It was missing the word "Joden" in the center. This was the Dutch word for Jews. When I see that yellow star in my mind's eye, I get a lump in my throat. My mother's friends convinced her to remove the stars. These were the children who disappeared. Did she want the same thing to happen to her children? No.

The Diary of Anne Frank is in the news. Rob and I watched a 60 minute documentary of an American retired FBI investigator who went to Amsterdam and was able to successfully find the likely informer.

My mother had a warm and welcoming personality. Everyone loved her, including me. She was kind and gentle. Her generosity was huge and took many forms. She gave of herself. Whether it was her knowledge, her time, her love, or her passion—she shared it. She was sincere and focused on whatever she paid her attention to. Mother loved taking walks with my sister or with me. During the walk, she would share a story, beloved to her, and usually a Greek one. She made every effort to look on the bright side of life, even when the going got tough. She was intelligent and had a good memory for detail. She taught definite beliefs and values. She believed in the equality of women. She enjoyed in depth discussions. She also participated in intellectual debates, as did my father.

She was well educated, motherly and nurturing to her children. She had her Doctorate in Latin and Greek languages. When my oldest siblings were toddlers, she taught for a few years to help my father finish his studies. But that was before I was born. She was a teacher through and through. She had expectations of each of her children. She was in charge of the staff in a large beige smooth stucco house, our house in Apeldoorn. There was a lovely large well- manicured park across the street that had a round pagoda bandstand where music played every Wednesday evening. (I actually never heard it because I was living in the country with my godparents.) She was an active member of a large extended family that got together every year. Even today, these members get together. Some even see each other formally TWICE a year! The entire family is very warm and welcoming and even today we are one big, happy unit with tolerance and loads of talent in various fields. Family members span the world, with a large contingent in Peru.

My godmother's name is Tante Jannie. I love her to distraction and she is with me in spirit today. I bonded with Tante Jannie. For the first five years of my life, I thought she was my biological mother. My earliest memory is of being cradled in her arms, as she was chatting with a friend or relative. I loved listening to the reverberation of her voice against my little ear. It gave me an all-encompassing sense of peace, comfort, love, patience, gentleness, pleasure and generosity. When I was going to sleep years later and feeling so sad, this was the memory that comforted me the most.

Tante Jannie was efficient, fast, strict, flexible and smiled and laughed a lot. She beamed her love at me every time I was near. It was radiant and warming. I could feel it before she even entered the room. She was a people person and was one of the nine brothers and sisters in her family. The entire extended family of brothers, sisters, parents, cousins, nieces and nephews was very close. Hers was a practical education combined with a wonderfully clear mind. While she had no significant formal education, that did not stop her from leaving a large footprint in life, influencing many people.

In 1955, she started working at "De Echoput," a beautiful and popular restaurant that was rebuilt into a classy hotel and restaurant today. It is now owned by the son, (and his wife), of the original proprietors. Tante Jannie helped raise this son and his two sisters as well, after I had moved to Canada. The original owners were very appreciative of all her loving skills and T.J. managed things when the family went on holidays and managed all, under the guidance of the owners, when they were at home. She did that until well into the 1990's.

Over the years, I have come to appreciate Tante Jannie even more. She "taught" me the most. Intrinsically, that is where the bonding was so strong. She had gifts that she never, in all her 92 years, discussed. I know that she was psychic. She had learned to keep a great deal to herself. She was not judgmental and at a very young age, I could see that as a gift. Jealousy was also not in her nature. She was fair and made a daily conscious effort to infuse fairness into her environment. She loved to cook and made wonderful meals for all who came to visit. She loved having visitors and focused on each visit being "gezellig", or cozy.

My father was a tower of a man. For his efforts in WWII, he received the King's Medal of Courage and Freedom after saving more than a thousand British soldiers, Allied troops, and many German soldiers as well. The Allies were the countries including the U.S., Canada, Britain and Australia, who fought the Germans and the Japanese. My father had been a surgeon in charge of the Dutch Red Cross in the triage unit for over a year in 1944-45, working tirelessly for the cause. He had deft hands and a photographic mind. Originally he had wanted to become an astronomer but, when he saw the clouds of war coming in the early '30's, he continued his education in medicine instead. I felt his emotion, his passion. This was not something that I realized until these last ten years or so. He may have hidden his very passionate nature from many people, but I saw and felt it. He seldom showed his emotions. It was safer that way considering the work he did. From the perspective of his personality, it was hard to say where the "man" stopped and the "doctor" entered the room. He was time- conscious. He was self-disciplined and had a great sense of duty. There were times when he "let go" with joy and pleasure, and my adrenalin would rise as I eagerly watched.

He played as hard as he worked. There were more than 5,000 books in his Dutch home and even more in Hamilton, Ontario, Canada, where we lived for ten years. Books were his pleasure. His children were his pleasure also, although he left our upbringing to our mother. He had a shell collection from all over the planet. Salt and sweet water shells and more were everywhere in each house we lived in. These were all carefully catalogued in thin wide and long, light colored, oak drawers that went from floor to ceiling. He had a sixteen mm camera set with which he documented our life in The Netherlands before we left the country.

My second father was a man named Oom Cees. In my heart, Oom Cees is my father. I bonded with him. He loved me and I loved him deeply in return. I knew it and felt it all the time. He was a large man with soft hands and an even softer heart. There were many times when he and I were together in a comfortable silence. He taught me just as many things as Tante Jannie did. They knew they could have no children of their own and, because of that, I was their child. Oom Cees was a well-respected man. He too, received a medal after the war. General Eisenhower presented him with the Medal of Freedom. It was a highly prized medal from President Truman of the U.S. that celebrated freedom and courage.

Oom Cees was patient and tolerant. He was very careful and very protective of me, doting even. He had a wicked sense of humor appreciated by all and was well educated; very knowledgeable about his field of hunting. His education included a detailed knowledge about all things living in the wild. He loved the woods and had a respect for the animals in his keeping as the Head Game Warden for the Queen of The Netherlands. I can still feel his love; he is with me in spirit today. He was reliable and aware, he taught me intrinsically and through his actions. For my family, this family of T.J., O.C. and myself, actions spoke louder than words. Oom Cees was very stable in his moods and personal flexibility; he could set the mood and the tone in a group with ease. He was a natural born leader as he observed more than spoke and was non-judgmental, like T. J.

Having four parents didn't seem all that strange to me. In fact, I thought I was lucky to have four people in my life, loving me so dearly.

Most of my friends only had two parents, and one home. I had two sets of parents and two warm homes in which I was welcomed. But that duality and difference in opinions and backdrop may have created something inside me that was conflicting and confusing. The notion of duality is based on the premise that there is seemingly an instance or situation compromised of opposition, or it is a contrast between two concepts or two aspects of something. For me, my four parents were each special in his or her own light. They taught me different things and introduced perspectives I may not have experienced on my own. They were all loving and caring in their own ways, and I am appreciative of all they did for me. But where I truly belonged in spirit was confusing. And to some degree, I believe it inadvertently birthed a duality inside me that eventually played some role in my depression.

The First Six Years

The first six years of my life were magical. They were filled with boundless joy and happiness. Life was not complicated. I was born just after the hunger winter of 1944-45, on March 5th, 1945, near the end of the Second World War. In later years, I would realize that that time period as a fetus compromised my ability to use my brain well. With malnourishment, the delicate brain does not receive all the nutrients it needs to reach the potential of a well-fed fetus. Months before I was born, the Allies made a pincer movement to liberate the Dutch but it took longer than expected. In September 1944, the Germans in command told my father to operate on the wounded. My father realized that he had the upper hand, given that he was the local surgeon with the expertise. My father said that he would only operate if he were allowed to operate on ALL the wounded soldiers of the battlefield who could be saved. They agreed and it was done.

As with my five older brothers and sisters, my father was the attending doctor for my mother as she birthed me. Weeks later when the Canadian Allies liberated our town, my mother was carrying me, a babe, near the stairs when a grenade came through the thick oak door, shooting a piece of shrapnel into the calf of my mother's left leg. It was so deep that my father had to remove the piece through the other side. My mother was laid up for weeks, but on May 5th, a peace treaty was signed that ended the war.

Tante Jannie was working for my parents as head of the household staff. She and Oom Cees had been married for three years and were not blessed with a child. Over the years they were unable to have their own biological child and were excited with the prospect of me being their "child." For Tante Jannie, this was the perfect time to ask my parents if she and Oom Cees could look after me continually. She would bring me back and forth to work and look after me on the evenings and weekends at "Het Aardhuis", their home in the woods. My parents saw this as a solution. They were actually very generous people. There was no foresight at this time that this arrangement would have such an impact on Tante Jannie, Oom Cees and myself just a few years later.

However, these early years were magical because of the way that I saw and experienced life. My imagination was unfettered in both the country and the city. Each day brought new discoveries and adventures. I enjoyed the duality of being a part of these two families thoroughly. The frequent adrenalin rushes and fast pace of life were what I was accustomed to. I was completely safe and protected and I felt no demands. My life consisted of following Tante Jannie everywhere when she and I were in town. Trips into the woods with Oom Cees were a routine, done in an open jeep three or four times a week. We would haul an open-backed trailer behind us that carried red beets for the wild boar. I loved watching the boars eat. During these feeding trips, we would travel mostly in comfortable silence to quietly approach and watch the deer. These animals were the kings and queens of the forest. My heart would leap with joy every time Oom Cees pointed out a group of deer in the distance. These moments were truly cherished. Monitoring in the forest was a part of the job.

We had two smooth haired dachshunds that added a joyous dimension to our little family. Sometimes, Tante Jannie and Oom Cees had a dog or two or three that they were boarding. These were kept mostly in cages (cleaned daily) in the shed, which was 15 by 15 feet with a well-made stone floor. With a successful hunt, one or two skinned rabbits would be hanging from the rafters. I can still see them hanging with my mind's eye. That same day, Tante Jannie would make these rabbits into a delicious stew. The sense was strong that this would be my life experience forever.

At the house in the woods, Tante Jannie and Oom Cees taught me that we lived in the "Bible Belt." This is a belt that runs from the north to the south of the Netherlands and it contains many spiritual or religiously devout Christians. We were a part of that, although T.J., O.C. and I didn't go to church. They both believed and taught me that the whole environment is God's church. They worshipped in the woods. They also taught me that we are all *allowed* to believe what we do. God is a very loving God. We are not to judge others or ourselves for our beliefs.

In later years, Tante Jannie told me I did not start talking until I was four years old. Before then, it was a babble and garble. Like many, I had my own language. Mine lasted a little longer than normal. Once when I was four, I was left in the city for the day, I still do not know why. But I remember every detail and in the late morning, I crossed the street to a mother with her two small children who were waiting for the bus. When the bus came I hopped on right behind the family, intending to go to "Het Aardhuis." This was a route that I knew well and I sat quietly in the back, expecting the bus driver to drop me off at the usual stop. When the bus had reached its final destination, the driver discovered me in the back and knew who I was. My father was a well-known man in town.

The driver phoned the house in Apeldoorn. Tante Jannie was called and soon I was with her at the Aardhuis, where I had intended to be in the first place.

On days when Tante Jannie worked at my parents' house, she and I came together and I stayed near her. We would go into town together to go to the butcher, the baker and the vegetable stores. Most of the time my oldest four siblings were at school so I seldom saw them. My sister who was two years older played with me sometimes. I remember both of us playing with the two girls next door; they were the same age we were. I saw my mother but paid little attention to her. My father was seen as an important man who I looked up to with awe in those years. Once the eight of us went to a professional photographer for family photos. We all saw the same man again when he came to our house years later to take family pictures inside and outside the city house. The first time that I really started to be a part of my biological family was on the trip to Canada.

However, once we had emigrated, I couldn't just "hop on a bus" to arrive home at the Aardhuis. I was desperate. No matter the extent of my desperation, my relief of being with my godparents in the woods where I belonged in spirit wasn't happening.

That dawning sent me into a deep depression. It began when I stood on the pier in Quebec City, Quebec, Canada and established itself over the years. For the first months, I was in shock.

It wasn't until I was in my 50's that I learned from Tante Jannie that my grandparents, the parents of my father, had paid for the trip of my return at nine years old; for a year. Because I was too young to travel alone, my two years older sister was in charge and travelled with me back to Holland. We went by boat when commercial flights were not available yet. My sister was seasick, confined to her bunk for most of the trip. I remember thinking that I really could have gone on my own. But I told this to no one: not then, and not later. At this point already, I was keeping a lot of my opinions to myself. It was my experience that, when I shared my opinions, the feedback (or response) made me feel worse. It was easier to say nothing. Saying less was a way of life for me. When I spoke, I was in more trouble than if I didn't.

It is not surprising that someone who is depressed says less than when they are feeling good. However, you can see by what I've written that saying less is not necessarily an initial indication of anything being wrong. I was taught a love that held no bounds in my first few years of life. My core values come from that. I learned feelings. I am a sensitive, feeling person who was given a strength of spirit at a very early age. I am happy and grateful to have received the blessing of four parents. This taught me to have a flexibility that I enjoy today. For decades, I saw having four parents as spiritually confusing. Who were really my parents in my mind? What was I allowed to say? How was I to avoid stepping on anyone's toes? It felt impossible with so many personalities, opinions and feelings.

I love my brothers and sisters. I have had heart to heart talks with all of them. The complexity of my feelings is no more relevant than theirs. Have they ever told me that they understood the extent of *my* duality? The issues that arose made the emigration for my siblings traumatic as well. My oldest sister and brother, Agatha and Gus, have passed away. I can "feel" their complete understanding when I "feel" their spirits.

The nature of duality is that it offers two seemingly different perspectives. For me, the duality present in my early years did just that. It was extremely exciting and meaningful for me to have two sets of parents from two different backgrounds. I appreciated it and valued it, but it also pulled my identity in a number of different directions. The difference between the two and the extended families created an overload inside that I never fully addressed until I was an adult. I am not saying I view this as a negative. Rather, I simply acknowledge that the duality that occurred early in my life certainly had an impact on who I am today.

Good, bad, or indifferent, even from a young age, my life had always felt like a push/pull.

The first six years of my life were special. They were unique and loving and totally innocent. But with our immigration to Canada, the usual, the familiar, the norm changed. It shot me down a dark path, one that took most of my life to truly recover from. With this book, it is my intention to help and be of service wherever I can be. This world is hurting. I believe that the pen is mightier than the sword. I have a voice. Writing to you in depth makes me vulnerable to your judgment. And yet I'm asking you to learn from what I'm writing. There are a huge number of people who are hurting each day. There was my own depression that I was exposed to after my biological family immigrated to Canada. I wasn't ready yet then for a whole new world. The same may be true for you and your life. Change is a constant variable. It will occur and be with us no matter where we go. For me, change led to a difficult scenario. But it did not have to. Through learning how to cope with change, and many other experiences in life, we become more adept to absorb and turn the negative into a positive.

During the first few years of my life, I learned an independence of self that was to later give me strength with my depressive feelings. I had already learned how to stand on my own two feet. I was already in the practice of analyzing my feelings to myself. I protected myself by seldom sharing how I truly felt. My family duality taught me how to compromise. Being compliant and flexible had served me well in the first six years of life. The curveball of the immigration was the one that overwhelmed me; it was the one from which I could never quite recover. My brothers and sisters were thrown that same curveball. Our predisposition to depression is genetic as well. My father's younger brother committed suicide in 1942, aged 31, he had a sensitive soul and didn't tolerate the oppression of war. My mother's older sister committed suicide at the age of 56, when she was told that she had bowel cancer.

After my own suicidal thinking started at the age of 11, I knew that I must keep these thoughts and struggles to myself. I didn't want to burden my family with my mental suffering. The extent of love that I had received in the first years of my life carried me through my first ten years. After that, I fell apart. In the pages to come, you will become part of my journey. To this point, you have learned much about my own duality, and soon you will learn about how that duality has very much defined my life. Together, we will journey through the mind of a completely depressed and suicidal woman; me. It may feel like a rollercoaster. But in the end, I broke free of this suffocating depression and learned to live a happy and meaningful life. If you are depressed, the same can be true for you or those that you love. I am comfortable in saying that through my journey you will gain insight and understanding into the mind of a sad person. You can be the difference; you can change. If I can overcome my duality, my depression, and my suicidal thoughts, you can too. The repetition in this chapter is deliberate. It is my intention to make myself very clear.

Curtain Call

- *Those who do not speak may understand love as an emotion and feeling. The only way to communicate love is by showing it to them through action.*
- *Showing love is at the core of what we can do for ourselves first, so that we can in turn, give it to others.*
- *Depression takes many forms. It can be seen through speaking too much or not speaking at all. Be aware of those you love and ask plenty of questions.*
- *Depression is rarely caused by any one experience. It is the culmination of life events.*

— *The roots of a loved one's depression may be entirely unknown. It may be nature; it may be nurture; or both.*

— *Exploring the possible roots of depression may shed light towards healing.*

— *Experiencing the emotions of those who came before you can help you with your own journey.*

CHAPTER 2

Marvelous Memories

What children are taught from generation to generation shapes their lives. The clouds of war can hang over a nation long after the fighting and the killing have stopped. How we deal with the events that we have experienced in our minds is what determines how we move on. My first six years (from 1945 to 1951) were the post-war years in Holland. Basic items were slowly becoming more available, but I was unaware of the changing environment, I had everything I needed. I had a huge sense of abundance.

The following stories are the wonderful, marvelous memories of my early childhood. I have carried these memories carefully inside my heart for all of my life. Many of these have not yet been shared, and it is here on these pages that I wish to tell you about my privileged, early years that were full of love. These stories will also illustrate my transition from happiness to depression; with that said, I have no regrets, and am only grateful to share these memories in the pages of this book.

Family

I was fortunate to be raised by two strong extended families. After 1945, the sense of mistrust that had developed during the war was slowly released. My older brothers and sisters were back in school, and I seldom saw them. The youngest in the family was actually my sister, not me, because I saw myself as the daughter of Tante Jannie and Oom Cees. The parental home was a beautiful beige stucco building. On one side it was a two story, and on the other side of the front, it was a three story well designed home. Each level of the three stories had a window on three bumped out sides, so that they all looked like bay windows, nine of them in total. There was constant activity in the house, which I avoided. I liked the quieter, smaller home in the country better. I never told anyone because it wouldn't be right for me to compare, but I couldn't help comparing in silence. There was abundance measured in different ways in both places, each with its benefits, but I preferred the peaceful life in the woods.

One of my regrets is that I have many memory blocks throughout my life; I wish I could remember more. I was aware by the time that I was four and five years old (1949-1950) that my thinking did not seem to be as good as others. It made no difference to me; I was happy and content. As long as I stayed at the Aardhuis with Tante Jannie and Oom Cees, I was safe. My life would stay simple. That way I would not be confronted by mental demands. I wanted to be an accepted member of my parent's family, but I did not feel like I belonged. This feeling of being on the outside was only clarified many decades later, after spending much time and effort meditating on my childhood.

I know now that I have a right to be who I am. I have a right to my own opinions. I am allowed to share with you how I feel and, in doing so, I have no intention of stepping on the toes of my brothers and sister who are very important to me. I love all three of them very much, just as I loved my oldest sister, Agatha and my oldest brother, Gus, who are no longer with us. We are, each one of us, so very passionate. *I* am passionate and I am allowed to be. So this has nothing to do with being bipolar. The following memories will help tell the story of how I became the passionate person I am today. Let me tell you here also that where you see my repetition is where I have focused my meditations.

Contests, Dreams, and Markets

Oom Cees took me into town one Saturday morning and entered me into a balloon contest. This balloon was filled with helium and my name and address were tied to the string; then the balloon was released. There were many other children there who also had balloons. The balloon that travelled the furthest would win a prize. What a feeling of freedom that released balloon gave me! I imagined it travelling very far south, carried by the winds. As it turns out, my balloon landed in Belgium, and I won the prize. It was a silver teaspoon with a doggie on it. I still have it today.

Twice a week, on Wednesday and Saturday mornings, it was market day in Apeldoorn. On Saturday we sometimes went to town to surf the market. We never knew what treasures we might find! Later, we would walk on, through the main town street. We walked past all the shops. We would play a fun game where T.J. and O.C. would lift me in the air. "One two three....wheeeeeee." Again! "One, two, three....wheeeeee." There would be at least three long swings of lifting me high. The excitement and love in the air thrilled me! We would go into the cigar store just to smell the cigars and tobacco. I loved the smell in the store almost as much as I loved the smells of the forest.

Many nights when I went to sleep, I would dream about the wild boar (varkens or wilde zwijnen). I dreamt that I walked among them, as one of them, enjoying a life of comfort and ease. In the fall, I would hear the trumpeting of the male deer, announcing their intentions, while I was falling asleep. It was a welcoming sound for all beings and it marked the beginning of the season. I slept in an alcove, on the other side of the attic room where Tante Jannie and Oom Cees slept. Some mornings I woke up early, and I was allowed to snuggle between them to cuddle and feel warmer.

Royalty

Sometimes Queen Juliana came by our house with her three daughters. On a hill, from where we could all view the grassy knolls, heather, and sand with a line of trees along the back, was a teahouse. This was a few hundred feet up the hill to the right side of our house. Tall mature trees, spaced well apart, lined the footpath. To the left of our house, on a much larger hill, with even larger mature deciduous trees, was "Aardhuis I." This cottage was built by Queen Wilhelmina, the mother of Queen Juliana, and is a tourist attraction for the Dutch today. Queen Juliana was the mother of Queen Beatrix, and Queen Beatrix is the mother of the current King, Koning Willem Alexander. Thus, the Queen visited with the oldest daughter, Princess Beatrix, the middle daughter Princess Irene, and the next daughter, Princess Margriet. The youngest daughter, Princess Marijke needed mental support and was usually left at home.

Princess Margriet was a year older than I was. Once, when they all came, Princess Margriet wanted to go on my swing and she declared her desire to me. I said she could, if she asked me nicely. The Queen laughed and I realized that this was an answer that Princess Margriet had not expected. Another time, we were all at the teahouse at dusk. There were no deer to be seen in the distance, and the Queen thought of a game. She had four candles, one for each of us (I was the youngest there). Whoever reached the bottom of the hill first with the candle still lit would be the winner. I ran down the hill with my lit candle so fast that it went out! "Oh no!" Not to be deterred, I ran into the house, grabbed the flashlight, and yelled, "I won!" My beaming flashlight was my "lit" candle at the bottom of the hill. We all laughed. I don't remember who legitimately won. I paid no attention beyond that victory. The Queen was a very gentle, loving, kind, down to earth lady. I was not aware that I was to realize her "station."

I don't remember the Prince (Prince Bernhard), the husband of the Queen, ever being in the house. For a time though, almost weekly, the guests of the prince would come in for an hour for Oom Cees's well known, home-brewed, fresh coffee before the hunt. The coffee was ground first with a hand-cranked grinder. I can picture the unit before my eyes today. It was 6" tall, with a 5" square light tan wood unit with a 4" metal crank that would go around and around, by hand. That grinding sound is imbedded in my mind. And the smell of those fresh beans, as they were grinding, was heavenly. I sat with my little arms folded over the cross bars of the rectangular oak kitchen table. I said nothing but the men knew that I was there. I loved it. I knew that these would be precious memories for me in my older age. In later years I would dream again and again about these beautiful moments and relive them with picture perfect clarity.

The men had discussions that I sensed were "high level" and private conversations. They had no idea that I was so impressed with them, even though I couldn't understand what they were saying. I felt their ambience and love. They were excited. They were going on a hunt. This activity was exclusive and it was a privilege; they knew it and they appreciated it. I realized that I was the only female in a room full of powerful men; I was aware and appreciated my privilege. When I realized that they were talking about me, I would giggle and one man in particular would pick me up and jiggle me on his knees. That man was the founder of Philips, where decades later, my son would be employed, and where he received his PhD in Eindhoven, the world headquarters. What a privilege. I remember Mr. Philips as a wonderful kind, laughing man who knew how to feel joy. True joy.

I felt like a real princess, and I saw no distinction between the princesses who came to visit and myself. I had been to their palace, too.

My sister and I were invited to play with the princesses because of my father's "station." I rode a tricycle down the long halls of the palace, but someone stopped me. I thought these grownups were "stiff" and unfriendly. There were too many rules for me. I asked Tante Jannie if I could please not go again. And so I never did. Neat, huh?

Childhood Delights

An empty spool of thread provided me with hours of entertainment. Four nails were hammered into the top of the spool. A wool thread was started with a crochet hook, and a braided length was created via hooking the wool over the nails. Many decades later, Tante Jannie told me that after I went to bed at night, each night she would unravel what I had done because we were low on wool. I never noticed.

The bus service used paper tickets. When all the tickets were used, a 3" by 5/8" strip would remain. Once the two staples were removed from this strip there were 12-15 pieces of paper, all exactly the same. I would glue each piece into a ring. The next piece was looped through the ring to add another ring. Thus, I could make a long string of joined rings. This activity was part of my birthday preparations once a year. Doing all this preparatory work added to the excitement. The bus drivers had been pleased to give me what otherwise would have gone into the garbage.

Some of my favorite memories are those of my weekly bath. Every bit of water was warmed on the kitchen stove. One big heavy pot was used. While the water was heating, (it had been pumped up), Tante Jannie would move over the big kitchen table. A big towel was laid on the linoleum floor. Then the large galvanized tub would be fetched from the shed. It received a wipe down. The water was brought in a galvanized pail to the tub from the sink. This was carefully poured into the tub so as not to spill a drop. After 2 or 3 pails full, a pot with a handle was used to scoop boiling hot water into the tub.

Tante Jannie always warned me to stay away; she said that the water was "too hot!" These steps were repeated until the tub was ¾ full. The whole ritual was done so that the final water temperature would be just right for me. She tested the water and swirled it with her arms. When it was the perfect temperature, she would say, "Now, dear treasure, you are allowed to step into the water." And with a big beaming smile, sending me love, she would wrap her arm around my entire body, and guide me over the rim. I would slowly glide into the perfect temperature water, as it rose up to my chest. Without a word, she would turn and get another half pan full of boiling hot water from the stove and very slowly and gently, add just a little more hot water to make it "just right" again. Over the next half hour, she would wash me all over with a bar of soap. Every 5 minutes or so, she would add a little more "hot" water to keep the temperature "just right." I loved my bath. It was very pampered and exclusive. And to think, this bath was given every week with tender loving care! I was so fortunate.

There was a complete sense of happiness and trust in our little home in the woods. Our family was complete. I was given as much freedom as I could ever want, within the parameters of knowing that my safety was paramount. Year after year, while in the city, there always seemed to be some social demand that accompanied being the youngest in a large family. Year after year, I was aware that my greatest happiness occurred in all the moments (and more) that I described from my childhood in the countryside, among the trees and wild animals.

Care and Concern

My happiness in the first years was complete and I did not question my feelings. I knew that I was happy. Every single day brought new excitement and adventure. My trust was secure, knowing that my protection was all encompassing. Once, T.J and O.C. and I were travelling by bus after visiting family. We were almost home and it was evening time. As usual, we sat towards the back of the bus. Someone came on the bus with a big bulldog on a leash and the dog decided to sit right next to me. Other people on the bus turned and looked because the dog was bigger than I was and had a fierce bulldog expression. My reaction to the dog, when I realized that he was there and decided to stay, was to mimic his expression. Everyone on the bus laughed. Their fear for me had vanished. The lesson here is to not be intimidated by appearances. When no fear is shown, it may well be that the danger disappears.

When I turned four, T.J and O.C. noticed my tonsils were getting larger. They were so large by the time that I was five that they almost occluded my throat. My father did the tonsillectomy and drove me immediately to T.J. and O.C. for the recovery. They had set up a large crib in the living room so that I was lying in comfort near them in the warm room. It was winter, and a wood stove heated the room. There was no central heat, and only the kitchen and living room were warm in the winter. My throat hurt. My father had not explained to me what he had done and why, so T.J. and O.C. explained what had happened. They made me a version of ice cream that was yummy. I don't know how it was made because fridges did not yet exist. Crushed clean frozen water was used, I think. I was told to take three big swallows at a time; then it would hurt less. I followed orders and they were right. I was angry with my father for not warning me about this event.

In hindsight, he may well have told me and it may not have registered. This was my first experience in learning how to forgive. My conclusion of this event is that the skill of forgiveness can be taught to a very young child. I was aware that I was a young child and I thoroughly enjoyed my position. My comfort in being a member of two families was complete. There was no controversy. My brothers and sisters were my family and there was no question for me as to why I wasn't with them all the time. My mother and father gave little indication at the time that their decisions were the final word. There was no need for me to question "who my parents" were. Life was simple. Life was good. Playtime with my sister and with friends were special events each time. It wasn't a routine. Playtime with my cousins (T.J's nieces) was a glorious event each time. These occasions would take some planning, and everyone regarded them as a big treat. The "nieces" were daughters of Tante Jannie's two sisters. Our family was close.

On occasions that were very rare, I played with my blood related cousins on my father's side: all of them lived in Hilversum. I had seven cousins, children of my father's two sisters. We had a wonderful big extended van Vierssen Trip family party in the summer of 1951. I didn't understand that this was a farewell party and that I was not to see anyone again for many years. My four oldest siblings were 13 to 19 years old. All four were very aware that this was a painful goodbye to our way of life in Apeldoorn. None have ever shared with me how they felt at that big party. An official photographer took a group photo. This event was, in hindsight, a very sad one. At first, in Canada, I wasn't able to understand that the loss of both large extended families added to my feelings of sadness. When I allowed myself to remember the pleasure of that family day, I made an effort instead to try and forget it. The memories were too painful. Memories like these plunged me into depression after the emigration. I told no one how I felt. I did not relate to where my siblings were emotionally. Alienation was more comfortable for me.

Saying Goodbye

After this party, I realized that we were going on a big trip; however, the realization that I would lose Tante Jannie and Oom Cees had not yet dawned on me. That I would lose both large extended families was devastating, but it was nothing compared to the loss of T.J. and O.C. Recently, my brother, Pieter, told me that two weeks before the emigration, he was asked to accompany my mother to visit Oom Cees. My mother had an important message to tell Oom Cees. It was then that Oom Cees was told that my parents had given it careful thought, and had decided that I was their (mother and father's) child and they would take me with them. It was a huge blow. There had been no previous indication that life would suddenly, drastically change forever. Oom Cees, whom I have never in my whole life seen crying, cried. It was then that Piete realized the significance and reality of what our nuclear family was about to undertake. Tante Jannie never shared with me what her reaction was; but I do know this: my loss for T.J. and O.C. not only rocked their marriage, it almost broke them apart.

Not until I was an adult did I hear several more stories. Dr. and Mrs. Winter, our neighbors in the city, came to the docks at Le Havre in France when the eight of us were leaving. Tante Jannie and Oom Cees were at the docks as well. Months before my oldest sister, Agatha, died in 1996, she told me of one memory that had haunted her. It was the emotional good-bye between Tante Jannie and Oom Cees and myself on that dock. She had never seen anything more heart wrenching in her whole life. Agatha had been treated for depression in the last decades of her life, and I wonder now what contribution our emigration had on her condition. We were all troopers. We did what we were told. We all loved our parents and each other. But we each carried a pain that had to be resolved individually within ourselves.

My brothers and sisters are all passionate, as am I. Keep in mind that I am providing my perspective of then and now. We each have a unique personality. Isn't that the case for everyone? Look for the positives in the personalities of children and foster them, for this is what contributes to healthy and positive growth.

There is one more story that I want to share at this time. On the trip to Le Havre, Oom Cees unwrapped a candy and gave it to me. This was a rare treat. It made me very happy. He put that wrapper into his pocket.

For the next two years, he kept that wrapper in his left pocket. Whenever Tante Jannie washed a pair of uniform pants, Oom Cees reminded her of the care she needed to take of that wrapper. It was carefully stroked until it lay flat, ready to go into a clean pair of pants that would be worn the next day. And so it continued. For two years. Think on this.

I know now that each one of us has energy. Each one of us can place our energy onto an item. What comes to mind are the hankies that were given to soldiers by their significant others before they left for war. I equate my candy wrapper to Oom Cees "feeling" my essence after I was gone. It gave him comfort. He "felt" my love. After two years, he was ready to let the wrapper go. And so it is for each of us. When something painful stops you from moving forward, let it go.

These six years were my magical years. There was a great freedom in feeling so secure in the family unit of Tante Jannie, Oom Cees, and myself. They loved me, I loved them, and the years revolved around our love. It was uncomplicated. There was no judgment; no expectations; no demands and no anger. I felt complete, and safe.

The freedom to explore all that the woods had to offer was a liberation that I would look back on with a painful sense of loss. The deer and the wild boar were in my spirit even when I wasn't looking at them. There, when morning coffee was outside on the patio and I had a cup of milk, I would explore nearby and often had a variety of beetles that I watched crawl over my little hands. They were my friends.

Before I go any further with my story, I want to reassure you that I have no regrets from any period of my life. Again, it is a humbling privilege to be able to share so much that I have kept inside. I do not fear your judgment. Anyone who isn't pleased or happy with me can just simply put down the book. My long disclaimer at the front of this book is meant to allow me a freedom of expression that I am thoroughly enjoying. I repeat: there are no regrets.

It is my strong spiritual belief system that I will share with you throughout this book that has guided me to overcome a lot of adversity. I am blessed with the wonderful husband that I have. And we are blessed with our three children and their families. It's all about families. Each of our children has a different belief system. My husband and I share our deep spiritual feelings, respecting each other's differences. We have all been given the freedom of choice. You may believe in the Universe. You may believe in God. We are all allowed to choose. I believe that God is a very loving God.

Curtain Call

- *Pay attention to the protests of a young child. Sometimes their intuition is telling you something important.*
- *Consciously make marvelous memories for your children and grandchildren. These are their foundation years. You are setting the groundwork for life patterns.*
- *Reward and respond to joyous behavior. All of us benefit from an attitude of gratitude couched in an environment of non-judgment.*
- *Avoid defensive and aggressive behavior. Give freedom of space within a safe surrounding.*
- *Forgive. Though it may be hard to do, it is poisonous to your body and mind to keep negative thoughts and emotions inside you.*

CHAPTER 3

The Challenging Immigration

With each day that our huge ship was on the ocean, my sense of being further and further away from my loved ones, my home, and my environment grew stronger. I know now that the immigration turned me into a hyper-vigilant person. And yet, strangely enough, I don't remember many details of the circumstances of the voyage. I don't remember the stateroom other than that it was small, with no windows to the outside. I felt trapped. As for whom I was with, where we ate, what activities there were on the ship, I have no memories.

The first memory that I can haul up is the one of watching our big light blue car being lowered to the dock from the ship by a crane with ropes. This 1950 Kaiser car that originally came from the U.S. was hanging in the air and it felt like it lasted forever. Then after going through some official procedures, we were all squeezed into the big car that would take the nine of us on land as part of our next journey. We were leaving Quebec City, Quebec, where we had just arrived in our new country, Canada.

On the Road

Our family bonded on this immigration voyage. The push was on to reach our new home. What comes to mind is this: one of the first video games that was invented (I think in the 1980's), was a game where there was a voice message that kept saying something like: "on target, we are on target." On this voyage, we were definitely "on target." My sister and I said nothing for the entire 3-day trip. We didn't drink much because we didn't want to prolong the voyage with having to make bathroom stops. It was a driving marathon. The weather was warm and perfect with no rain. No one spoke much except for the two drivers. After 12 hours of driving with 2 brief breaks for the "necessities," we would start looking for a suitable place to sleep. We were looking for a "Vacancy" sign. There was a bonding when that was the first thing we all looked for and someone spoke up if they saw a potential cheap, clean motel. We stopped around 9 or 10 p.m. The cheapest ones were the ones with little separate cabins. Early in the morning, we were on the road again. By this time, I was in total shock, but I am very grateful and glad that I have these memories to share with you.

We drove and drove. Last year, when Pieter and I were remembering together, he said that not only were we all crammed into the back, but also that the experience was made worse by the fact that we had a unit of blood with a pump and supplies. There was a constant watch required to keep the blood viable. It was on ice and the ice was repurchased as it melted. All this equipment was available for my father, who was suffering from a stomach ulcer that could bleed at any time and that would necessitate a transfusion. All the blood and supplies were kept behind the driver's seat and this added to the challenge of finding comfort in an already cramped car. The older ones took turns, but whoever sat behind the driver would have to endure hours of sitting sideways.

When we drove through Ontario on the Trans Canada Highway, I liked the province immediately. There were lots of trees, deciduous trees and various coniferous trees, and I felt right at home. But we kept on driving, and I was silently horrified. An expanse of fields opened up before us as the miles sped by. I felt an intense dislike for this new experience. The prairies of wheat fields seemed to stretch forever and I didn't like the smell. I longed for the woods.

I told this to no one in the car, but instead did my first active envisioning. In the back seat, silently, where no one was noticing, I let my mind comfort me. I was envisioning my father's office less than a month earlier. The examining table was tucked into a corner where an antique Chinese wood pattern privacy screen could be unfolded when called for. I thought this was forbidden territory, and so I only went in when no one noticed me. In my vision, I took several long glorious sniffs. I loved the smell. It was a very distinct pervasive smell of ether. I felt a sense of sadness and regret. I knew that this was a scent that I would not be enjoying again. At the age of just having turned six, it dawned on me that we were leaving our home and the town of Apeldoorn forever.

I have no memories or thoughts of the actual last embrace of Tante Jannie and Oom Cees on the dock in Le Havre, France. I know now that shock allowed me to move forward into the direction I was led. In later years, I discovered that they had experienced an adult sized shock as well. We are generally blessed with having painful memories blocked, unless we actively work at torturing ourselves with remembering them.

Getting Lost

We stopped in Regina two days into the voyage and visited some friends of my parents. I saw a tricycle outside and thought, "A-hah! This is my opportunity!" I hopped on the tricycle and started pumping my little legs. "Yes! Free!" I rode my bike and got lost. There were little lanes that confused me. These were the alleyways of North America that I had never before encountered; everything was unexpected. I came across what looked like a corner convenience store and looked up: three stone steps and a glass front door with two large storefront windows on each side. A tall, kind looking man came out and spoke. His voice and speech intonation were kind. I trusted him, but I couldn't understand a word that he was saying. "How can that be?" "Where am I that I don't understand what he's saying?" I started crying, even though I had rarely cried in my life up to that point. I hadn't even cried when I got a 6" long, deep gash in my right leg the year before when I was caught in barbed wire at dusk, near the Aardhuis. It was so far away; I knew that, as I stood there and cried. The amount of sadness that I was feeling was enormous. It was hard to bear. The stranger slowly reached out his hand towards mine and I took it. He guided me into the store. Another man, behind a counter that was a foot higher than I was, smiled. I felt reassured that I was in good hands.

Two young men in police uniforms came in and escorted me into their cruiser. This was a new experience and I liked it. I could trust these men. I had faith, and I felt safe. This was the first time that I accessed the great amount of faith that would be called upon to get through my depression. We rode around the blocks in the cruiser. I was sitting in the middle between these two trusted men. I could feel their empathy. It was a relief. No matter how long it took for them to find my family, my "new" family, I was safe. I remember my mother coming to the cruiser, smiling and laughing and speaking this strange language. Soon, I was out of the cruiser and that is where my memory stops. In later years, my mother told me that she knew that I had gone off on the tricycle. She had trusted me to have no problem being on my own because she knew that I had a good sense of direction. That was true, but that sense of direction had betrayed me this time. My mother had understood and had forgiven me for getting lost.

My next memory is of playing on the dirt streets in Moose Jaw, Saskatchewan, Canada. This was our end destination and we were to live in Moose Jaw for the next 10 months. It was a town that existed because the Canadian National Railway Line went through it. There were huge grain bins that filled the railway cars, and then the train moved on. Today this Company is called the Canadian National. My sister and I played a game where we counted the number of rail cars that rumbled by each day. Most of the time there were over 100, and that excited us. My sister and I met several boys and girls our age playing on the street. There were few cars on the road in the middle of the day. We were right in town and our road was not paved. I felt like we had arrived at the end of nowhere. I felt lost again. My sister was happier than I had ever seen her, and that didn't make sense to me.

Silence

On our street where my sister was so happy, I felt lost. My sadness grew. The switch had been activated and I was spiraling into a depth of sad emotion that was foreign and unknown to me. I realize now that I may have moved into becoming bipolar at the age of six, which is pretty hard for me to fathom. I stopped talking. I'm told that I had enuresis again, but I have no memory of the setback. But I remember being on a strike of silence. It was a peaceful protest on my part. No one even noticed. "Ok," I thought, "So be it." For all of August, all of September, all of October, and into November, I was very comfortable with not saying a word. It was a form of preserving myself. No one needed to know how I felt, especially if they didn't even notice. "Who cares?" Well, I knew God did. I knew that He cared. This was when I first silently counted on God, and the Trinity, to carry me through.

As soon as we had settled in Moose Jaw, sixteen crates arrived from Quebec City. Each standard crate was a cube, which was measured at 8' by 8' by 8'. We purchased some wood and started to build an aluminum trailer that we would haul back to Ontario the next summer and live in for a few months while our parents were deciding where to purchase the next home. It would be where my father would set up his Canadian medical practice. This was before the days of OHIP ("Ontario Health

Insurance Plan"), the socialized medical plan for the province. I helped with building the small trailer. It slept four people. I enjoyed screwing in the screws on the floor with an electric drill. It was the first time that I held a power tool and I liked it. I appreciated the trust that was extended to me by allowing me to help and participate. I did this with joy and excitement. Mind you, I did this in silence. *"Remember what peace there may be in silence." (Desiderata)*

In Moose Jaw, I was put in senior kindergarten, as I was considered to not be ready for first grade. My oldest sister was gone to the University of Saskatchewan in Saskatoon to study medicine. She was in her first year. My two older brothers were working on oil rigs in northern Saskatchewan. They said that it was back breaking work, and they were sending most of their pay back to our father. My youngest brother, Oncko, was boarding with a lady somewhere in Moose Jaw who became like a second mother to him. He had a big paper route after school, and he's described how hard it was to deliver all the papers when there was a biting cold wind. None of us had ever experienced such an unexpected exposure to a cold climate like this. My parents and my sister and I lived in a small one-bedroom basement apartment. This was the rental that we could afford. My father earned a bit of money at the local hospital, and studied a lot at the little kitchen table. The lighting was poor. The little bedroom had two bunk beds and mother and I had the bottom bunks.

What I remember about my kindergarten class is not the students, but rather the teacher. The teacher had asked my mother to come to the school and meet with her because she was concerned about my silence. She had not yet heard me speak one word and thought that something was seriously wrong.

My mother said that I talked sometimes at home, so according to her my silence at school was psychologically based. What I remember next is being alone under a table in the middle of the classroom. The students were sitting cross-legged, around and about, but with a large empty diameter of a circle around me. In other words, I had a feeling of space. I was under the table and I had lots of space. The table was my shelter and the students were safely at a distance. I imagined that I was in a play and that I was a cat. My role was to meow at the appropriate time. I obeyed my cue, and I loudly meowed. Suddenly I was "BUSTED"!!! From then on, there was no point in my staying silent. Everyone knew that I had a voice. I participated in everything in that class for the rest of the year.

The trailer was built and ready for the trip in early July of 1952. The 16 crates that were behind the house where we rented our basement apartment, were out there all winter, and then they were shipped to Hamilton in the fall of 1952. This was my first Canadian winter and I was cold. There was no basement window to open at night to let in fresh air. When we went out during the day, there were many times when it felt like it was too cold for me to breathe comfortably. It helped to have a thick, long scarf around my neck, draped over my mouth and nose. A year later in 1953, Patti Page came out with the song, "How Much is That Doggy In the Window? The One With the Waggly Tail?" I resonated with that song, so very much. I missed my two little brown wiener dogs. I felt very much alone, yet I had God with me to give me comfort. I told no one. Who would understand the level of comfort that I received from something that can't be seen? Also, I feared rejection, were I to share that very private and personal comfort.

Every day, Tante Jannie and Oom Cees were in my heart. I felt like I was with them in spirit. I knew nothing about the wrapper that Oom Cees had in his pocket. I went to sleep at night, standing at the Aardhuis's green wooden front door with Tante Jannie and Oom Cees comfortably housed inside. Later, in these same dreams that I dreamt over and over again, I would be in the woods with the boar, feeding them, feeling comfortable. I was one of them. When in the morning I awoke, reality struck me anew every time. There were no trees in Moose

Jaw. The air didn't smell the same. The extended families of all four of my parents were left behind in Holland, and I wondered how long I could keep going like this. I told no one of any of this torment, not then and not over the following years. I never shared the extent of my emotional pain. During this period of my life, it felt like time stood still; it felt as if the agony was lasting forever.

Once in the fall of 1951, when I had a booboo on my knee from bumping it into the bunk bed furniture, I cried in despair of the circumstances that we were in. My father was kind, since he thought it was just the booboo that I was crying about; I didn't correct him. He looked me in the eyes and showed kindness, love, and empathy. He had a Band-Aid for me that he unwrapped and put on. He smiled, stroked my shoulder in comfort, and with his index finger of the right hand pointed upward. Looking at me and then looking up, he said, "Look, there goes the pain," "It's gone to heaven, see?" And I was amazed. Believe it or not, that booboo pain was completely gone! Vanished! How did that happen?

Changes

To this day, I consider the experience as a confirmation that I can trust in God's miracles. Please note that by saying this I am expressing myself in that way that I feel most comfortable. I hope that my honesty and sincerity does not knock you out of synchronicity with my message. I believe that you can hold your own beliefs, and while they may be different from mine, you can still gain something from my story. Please insert what you are comfortable with, when my words do not strike a chord. You may very well regard "the source" as just what is out there in the universe, and that is fine. I know God accepts that belief. I want this story to fit your belief system. All living things hold energy, and you and I are energy sources. I believe that we are moving towards all 7 billion of us human beings becoming "ONE." I believe that this is part of God's plan.

He knows how this universe is unfolding, for He is "yesterday, today, and tomorrow." And He loves each one of us more than we can imagine. I am finally at peace with the love that I am receiving, and I am bursting at the seams with my desire to give that love to you.

This is at the core of how the immigration changed me. When I felt alone in the middle of nowhere at six, I felt the love that is available to all of us. The decision of who came into my life from then on was left in God's very capable hands. Moving with my biological family, where I "belonged," was a part of God's plan for me. I understand what He wants for me, and now it is up to me to fulfill that plan. You can do this too. As you're reading, keep in mind what has happened in your life that needs some closer self-analysis. The reason why I say this is because you know yourself better than anyone else. You can do this! As we move forward in this book, I will share with you some tools that brought me to the recovery that I am enjoying today

Children are the same today as I was back then. That's why I'm asking you to look back and figure out where your thinking got stuck. If you are a professional, this is how you can help reluctant, quiet children. The greater the trauma, the longer it may take for the child to trust you; however, with persistence, you can break through and truly help them.

My relationship with God grew day by day. I felt God was with me. I was not alone. I felt love and peace. Even though I was struggling with the emotional upheaval caused by the immigration, I knew this was God's plan for me and I was content with it. I felt that if I kept my bond with God a secret, then it would be a bond that no one could destroy. This was when I started letting my inner light shine again. I let it glow just a little bit.

I was being true to myself. In June of 1952, our new Queen (Elizabeth II) ascended to the throne of England. She had just lost her father, while she was away in Africa. I could relate to that. I had also lost my spiritual father and mother in the past year. There was lots of news coverage, and I soaked it all up. I felt more of the abundance. The world wasn't so unpleasantly big for me anymore. The news came to us from across that same ocean that I had travelled and I realized that we were not in the middle of nowhere after all. The traumatic emotional blow of the immigration was difficult for me to overcome, yet I was comfortable in carrying my sadness without sharing it.

Power and Peace

I have realized in this past year that when we speak, we give our voice power in the universe. The same is true with the written word. Writing down and sharing our stories creates a power that goes out into the universe. I want you to try and feel the power. I expect that doing this will empower you to let go of the burden that you are carrying. Finding God is the greatest gift that I have ever received. I would be a complacent, apathetic adult had I not overcome all the challenges in my life. I certainly would not be feeling all the love that I do today.

There was no choice for me when my parents immigrated and took all 6 of us out of our comfort zone. We all had to absorb and face our challenges in our own way. I discovered first hand the variety and depth of emotion demanded for this life changing experience. There were times when I thought, "Ours is not to question why, ours is but to do and die." These were the thoughts that I seriously started to struggle with just 5 years later. In the meantime, I was coping; the alienation that I felt with my "new" family was blunted by my wonderful deep relationship with God. "I am with you, always." This was the thought that played through my mind year after year. It gave me peace, love and hope. This led me to knowing that whether or not I had immigrated to Canada, this was the path I was meant to be on. Today, I still know that God is in charge. I follow His lead. This is the peace that I have found. You will find your peace in whatever form you are meant to, as long as you keep looking. Have hope and keep searching until you find your peace.

Curtain Call

– *We are blessed to have the ability to go into shock when a life experience becomes too painful. Sometimes the feeling of shock is deliberately chosen, and sometimes the transitional thinking is done "for" us.*

– *Look for your spirituality to guide you to coping mechanisms.*

– *Mental health is a large and serious issue. I want to make a contribution to improving mental health. My level of expertise is drawn from my personal road of recovery.*

CHAPTER 4

School Days

The following stories are taken from memories of my school days, both in Canada, and in The Netherlands. These were formative years for me, and many of these experiences have had a profound effect on my life.

In late June of 1952, the four of us, my mother, father, sister and I, travelled from Moose Jaw, Saskatchewan to Stony Creek, Ontario. When we were halfway, in Winnipeg, Manitoba, the three of us waited while Father wrote the exam that would allow him to practice medicine in Canada. He had told us that he could not afford to fail because the expense of studying for another year would be prohibitive. There was extra pressure on him because most doctors needed to study for two years before passing these exams. Our father was very grateful when he succeeded in getting his license that day.

My sister and I were in the trailer for the entire trip to Ontario while our parents were sitting in the Kaiser (car). There were no seat belts in the car or in the trailer because these were not invented yet. We never questioned why our parents had us in the trailer instead of in the car with them. In hindsight, for all of us to be in the car would have been safer; but times were different then, and people didn't question things the way they do now.

We arrived and settled in a trailer park in Stony Creek with an air of adventure. My sister and I both discovered that we liked being in this new province. Within a few weeks, we moved to an apartment on Bay Street in downtown Hamilton. We started school nearby, but before the year ended, we were established at our permanent address in Hamilton at 780 Main Street East. It was a large, comfortable 18- room, three story red brick house on the corner of Main and Blake Street. Over 10,000 cars sped by the house every day because it was the main thoroughfare. These were the days before the four to eight lane divided highways. There was a stoplight one block earlier, which made it easy for us to cross the street. We waited for the traffic and that was when we learned to go with the flow.

Marnie

The only thing that I remember about those first three years is the wonderful friendship that I had with Marnie. She lived three short blocks away from me and we were inseparable. Either we were at her house, or we were at mine. Her older sister was conveniently the same age as mine, so this was a double bonus. Marnie and I went to Brownies together, every Tuesday. I was a "sixer," which is someone who is a leader for her peers. A sixer has five Brownies who stand behind her at the beginning of the meeting as we all read

"The Brownie Promise"

I promise to do my best:
To be true to myself, my beliefs and Canada
I will take action for a better World
And respect the Brownie Law

This was a highlight of my week. I loved the responsibility of guiding my peers. Brownie meetings were held in the basement of St. Giles Church, and that had me feeling right at home. Being a Brownie allowed me to become more comfortable and trusting with other girls my age.

In my bedside table is a precious index card, leaf green colored, that I have saved from these meetings:

"A Brownie Prayer" Dear Father in Heaven

We know we are Your children,
We want to serve You faithfully,
We want to keep our Brownie Promise.
Help us to listen to Your voice;
Help us to be willing and quick to do Your work;
Help us to be friendly and loving,
And help us to thank You every day
For all Your gifts to us.

Amen.

What I loved about Marnie was that she was kind and generous. We shared all our secrets and we could trust each other. The feeling of belonging that came with having Marnie as my friend was something that I cherished. The edge was taken off my loneliness.

We loved the freedom that we had to come and go as we pleased. Today, parents need to keep a closer watch on their young children because the world is not as safe as it was sixty years ago. As a wonderful surprise, Marnie and I found each other and re-connected just a few short years ago, and we're enjoying our friendship all over again. When Marnie and I go over our memories now, she enhances what I remember and vice versa. It's fun to recount all our adventures and rekindle our friendship.

Letters

I'm realizing now, that there were very few letters shared between Tante Jannie and myself. When I revisited Holland at the age of nine, I asked her about this when we were together again. She said that she was not a writer and I fully accepted this explanation. I'm also realizing that if T.J. and O.C. had written me letters, they would have been opened and read by my mother. T.J. and O.C. would have known this, and since both of them did all they could to avoid confrontation, they didn't write often. Both Oom Cees and my father have never written me a letter. This contributed to my sadness because it made me feel like they thought I wasn't worth their time. My mother wrote sincere, long letters that I would read over and over again to get the most out of them. The rare letter that I received from Tante Jannie, I treated like gold!

Twin Beds

My sister and I were dressed the same, just as we were when we lived in Holland, for a special trip to Rochester, New York, one early fall weekend in 1952.

Friends of our parents, John and Dot Livermore lived there. Our parents' friend, To Faber, was another Dutch-American who was also there for the occasion. We had a wonderful well-cooked, homemade meal and then slept in a luxurious bedroom upstairs. My sister and I had our own room with twin beds and matching bedding; I felt an abundance that I hadn't felt in over a year. Yet, I still missed my godparents so very much. Before I went to sleep every night, I would magically place myself at the Aardhuis.

Jesus Loves the Little Children

In 1953, I started to go to Ryerson United Church, a few blocks further east of our house. Every week, I went alone to the 11 a.m. service. My parents were fine with my decision to go alone. Going to church gave me a tremendous sense of homecoming. The routine of the service was so very comforting. There were usually as many as 200 in the congregation. I always sat in one of the back left pews. Ryerson United Church had a surrounding balcony where some of the congregants sat. Halfway through the service, I went to the Sunday School downstairs. It was the highlight of my week. I went home every time with a little 4-page picture pamphlet that made me feel so rich. Around once a month, one of the hymns sung in the main church was "Jesus loves the little children, all the children of the World, red and yellow, black and white. They are precious in His sight. Jesus loves the little children of the world." After I had heard that hymn a few times, it was part of my routine to sing it silently to myself when I was going to sleep at night. If I started to think about Tante Jannie and Oom Cees, I would burst into tears. No one benefitted from me feeling sorry for myself, so I would quash it by singing that hymn.

Reunited

One day, I was told that my sister and I were returning to Holland for the next school year. I was over the moon with happiness! In mid- June 1954, the departure date arrived and our parents drove us to New York City. My sister and I were settled in our berths and the adventure began. For most of the ten day trip, my sister was seasick. She stayed in our stateroom every day except for the first and last day. That left me to explore and enjoy the ship on my own, and I loved it! I was going home! Tante Jannie and Oom Cees, and Dr. and Mrs. Winter (our parents'

Apeldoorn neighbors) were at the dock when we arrived. I was brimming with happiness. Dr. and Mrs. Winter took my sister in their car and that was the last time I saw her for the next year. Saying good-bye to my sister was a blur because I was completely focused on the re-union with Tante Jannie and Oom Cees.

For a whole year, Tante Jannie and Oom Cees and I would be together! But first, I was to go on a family holiday with my cousins and their parents (my father's sister and her husband). I was deeply disappointed that no sooner were Tante Jannie, Oom Cees and I together, we would be ripped apart again! The three of us said nothing to each other about the holiday, not then and not later when we were finally by ourselves. One of the things that T.J and O.C. taught me was not to complain about the turn of events. As difficult as it was to bear, this was when I first realized that there was no such thing as "coincidence." It was at this time, during the first two weeks of July 1954, that I silently did a lot of contemplating. I needed to make sense of why I was constantly exposed to so much emotional pain. Of course I was excited about going to Switzerland with my cousins, but this was happening at the expense of my great need to be back with my "parents." No one knew about the extent of my emotional turmoil. Even when I started living with Tante Jannie and Oom Cees, I said nothing about my recent emotional roller coaster.

The Swiss Holiday

Tante Annette, Oom Koos, Jan Pieter, Kieke and Jacob, Petra and Saskia, and Oom Koos's cousin and I were going by train to Switzerland for a two-week holiday high in the mountains. We children were five cousins and myself: two boys and four girls. We sang a favorite song over and over to break the monotony of the long train ride. "We zijn der bijna, we zijn der bijna, maar nog niet helemaal." This means, "We're almost there, we're almost there, but not quite yet." It's a catchy tune. On the day that we arrived, there was flooding and the bridge over which one would normally get supplies was washed out. For the entire two weeks, every second day was devoted to Oom Koos and his cousin going for 2 hours down the mountain, and back up for four hours to keep the 9 of us well stocked with food and sundries. We were in a real, functioning Swiss Chalet, with the owner and his wife gone with their cattle for higher summer grazing. The days were beautiful, there was no rain, and we went on short treks.

One time, we were all in a big, clear, shallow water puddle. The smooth rocks fascinated me and I bent to pick one up. Oops! Oom Koos and I bumped heads! He got a headache and was in bed for the rest of the day. He said that I had a very hard head, yet there was no anger in his statement, and I was amazed. I loved him all the more. On the days that there were no supply trips for him, we children tried to convince him to take us on trips up the mountain. One day he did have the strength to say "yes," and we gloriously breathed in the fresh mountain air, and made tracks in the snow.

Holland

During the school year in Holland, I was put in grade 3. This grade was chosen because it best suited my level. I loved being in school in Holland. The day was very structured and each student was made to feel special. This was the year that I learned how to knit as one of my class subjects. I loved all the subjects, and had no trouble socializing. I loved (and still love) to socialize. At recess, I gravitated to the children who were playing with marbles in the dirt. A little hole was dug out, circles were made in the dirt, and beyond the widest circle, about a foot in diameter, we took turns getting our marble into the hole. It was knocked in with our thumb and forefinger. These marbles had names, and several kids were fortunate enough to have a BIG one. These big marbles were twice the size of the rest and had more powers. The bell always rang before we were finished, so we had to let the game go and run to our seats in class. This was when learning to "let go" started coming to me with ease.

Stropje

I took the V.A.D. bus to and from school. I was allowed to get on and off the bus on my own after a few months, but in the beginning Oom Cees walked me to the bus stop and waited with me until I hopped on. On the way home, I would round the bend for the last 50 yards and every time my dog, Stropje, would come running towards me. His happiness echoed my own—this routine was heaven. The 2 dachshunds of my toddler days were no longer alive, but Stropje more than made up for the loss. Stropje was a wire-haired Jack Russel with the most wonderful, loving personality.

Piano

When the school year started, so did my weekly piano lessons. Mrs. Van K's lessons started on Wednesdays directly after school; she lived within walking distance so I walked alone to her house near the Loolaan. She had a son who was in his early twenties and one day, for some reason, we were alone in the room. The lesson hadn't started yet, and he asked me if I would please sit on his lap because he was feeling cold. His mother kept the house cool because (I think) she couldn't afford the cost of heating it well. Once I was on his lap for a few minutes listening to his soothing, gentle voice, he asked me if he could put his hand on my nice warm tummy because his hands were so cold. I was a complete innocent. At that point, I was not aware of his further intent. I approved having his hand at waist level but I watched my tummy in horror as he was lowering his hand and then I watched him quickly and easily put his hand under my pants, against my skin and continue to go lower, very fast. I jumped up before he could reach my privates. I took my books and ran out of the house! I caught the next bus and then ran home.

I told Tante Jannie what had happened and asked if I could please never go back there again. T.J. explained to me that there are men in this world who have no respect for women. She was very sorry that this had happened to me, and she assured me that I was right to run away. She phoned Mrs. Van K., told her what her son had done, and said that I would not ever be back. That was the end of taking piano lessons until I came back to Canada. I never told my parents or my brothers and sisters this story. My lessons were restarted in Hamilton. Even then, it was difficult to take lessons because the memory of this trauma kept revisiting me over and over. Still, I chose to keep the emotional trauma of the event to myself.

Returning

The wonderful hiatus year in Holland would be looked back upon with sadness when I returned to Canada because even though the Canadian school system was good, I felt more in tune with the Dutch style of learning. Plus, it also hurt to leave T.J. and O.C., and all the new friends I had made. To help remember the new friends and the family that I was saying goodbye to, they all wrote goodbye notes to me in a Poisie album that I still have in the drawer next to my bed. When I was feeling lonely back in Hamilton, I would pull it out and let the messages comfort me. In the early summer, our year together was over and saying goodbye was not as hard as the last time. We had said goodbye before and survived, so we would survive again. At this point, I was older and more capable of understanding time lines.

When I arrived back home, it was an exciting time. My brother and sister performed a moving play about our great grandparents in the back yard of 780 Main Street East. At the time, everyone saw a bright and confident future ahead. That was the summer of 1955. I looked for my friend Marnie, but she was not at our school anymore. It was a loss that didn't stop me because I had already adapted to so much change. The year with Tante Jannie and Oom Cees had given me a refreshed and renewed outlook. I felt confident, happy, and ready to weather the storms. I had loads of energy.

Babies

For the ten years that we lived at 780 Main Street East, about 800 babies were born at our house. My father had a maternity clinic in our home. These were the years from 1952 until 1962, when the arrival of OHIP put a stop to our clinic. I remember women screaming on occasion. It was a part of life. There were no caesarians necessary, ever. Sometimes, with a difficult birth, forceps were needed to assist with the birthing. Everything was meticulously sterilized. Father had several sets of variously shaped forceps. The shape concept was the same for each one, though. The baby's head would be gently cradled inside the forceps, and during a "push" contraction, father would gently pull and guide the baby out. Sometimes the baby had to be "turned" before birth, a difficult procedure. This was only explained to me, as I was not privileged to watch such adult affairs.

It was the task of my sister and me to bring the patient's meal trays up and down the two flights of stairs in our home clinic. We were taught to have a professional manner, and to be friendly, kind and not over-exuberant. I smiled a lot. I loved serving these happy new moms. On occasion, we were offered, and allowed, to hold their firmly wrapped newborn babies in our arms. My love for these little babies knew no bounds. On one walk with my mother, I promised her that when I was grown and married, my husband and I would have 25 babies and we would build a house right next door so that we could look after her and father. My mother chuckled and looked down, smiling. She told me that she knew there would be no way that I would want 25 children when the time actually came.

Treatments

In September of 1955, when I went into grade 4, I was the tallest and the oldest in my class, which was embarrassing. My mother took me to an Ear, Nose, and Throat Specialist because a routine hearing test showed that I had a significant loss. It seemed as though I was headed to a school for the deaf. Instead, the specialist gave us hope by suggesting that the excessive earwax that I produced would be reduced if I had nine 1-minute radiation treatments on each ear (18 minutes total). For the next nine weeks, I went to the hospital for these treatments. I remember the huge machine above my head, with my ear in the crosshairs. I was not allowed to move during that minute. The treatments worked and I went into grade 5, Miss Vail's class. In that class was Cheryl, who became my new best friend. She included me in all that she was doing, and I was overjoyed. We went to baton twirling and tap dance classes on Saturdays. The studio was downtown and we went by bus. Cheryl was able to convince the teacher that I would keep up with the students who had already taken tap for years. I did keep up, no problem.

Just recently, Cheryl and I have discovered that we both had the same radiation treatments for the same duration (9+9=18). After these treatments, I had the added problem of the entire area behind both ears and on the ears being open with excoriation. For months, this area remained broken, bleeding, and coated with puss. I would pick off the newly dried puss that was sitting on the skin because it was itchy. Then when the scabs were gone and it was bleeding, I would feel pain. No matter what treatment my father prescribed, it did not heal. Out of desperation, my father drove me to a patient of his who lived on the Mountain. Hamilton is a horseshoe shaped town with Lake Ontario on the north side and "the Mountain" on the south; to the east lays Stony Creek and to the west lays Burlington.

The patient's name was Alie and she was a fascinating woman. She had the gift of supernatural healing, and was a psychic, used by the police to successfully solve and find missing children and other difficult cases. She had me sit on a stool, and then she proceeded to slowly circle me with my eyes closed; next, she "clicked" her fingers near each of my ears. After being with her for 2 weekends and getting several of these "treatments" from her, my ears were completely healed! It was then that I was initiated to the making of miracles. I am still so grateful for her.

Fruits of Labor

In the late spring of 1956, I helped empty a room full of dirt. The "new room" was a part of the basement, and the space was to become a workshop. I was glad to do something really helpful for my parents. It was hard work though; the wheelbarrow could only be just half full of dirt, or I wouldn't be able to move it. I would push it up the ramp over twelve steps into the back yard. Every weekend, I would do some loads because I liked the physical labor and I liked being helpful. That summer my sister and I started fruit picking for the season to make extra money. We did this every summer for five years, except for when I was in camp. On Saturdays, we would take the bus to a mall parking lot where farmers came in at 6 a.m. to choose the workers. We picked raspberries, strawberries, cherries, and apples. When I was older I was taken further afield to pick peaches in season. This paid more because picking peaches was a delicate job.

I was privileged to go to fourteen summer camps between the ages of 10 to 14. Most of the camps lasted about two weeks. My mother was the one who organized my registration, and it turns out that they were mostly church related, which made me happy. These weeks taught me many lessons; I was considered a leader every time, which was a huge boost to my morale.

After my eleventh birthday, I started remembering the joy of the previous year and I became unbearably upset. Week after week, it was harder for me to cope with the reality of being in *this* family instead of the one where I was so happy. I knew that it did not make sense. I wasn't coping with the amount of sadness I was feeling. I knew that I was alienating myself from everyone around me, except Cheryl. But Cheryl wasn't with me at home when I was feeling the gut-wrenching sick depression. I shared this with no one. Sharing my struggle with my family would make the sadness all the harder to bear. I knew that there would be little sympathy for me because I would simply be sharing the details of their own struggles. I envisioned them telling me that my woes were no worse than theirs, or anyone else's.

It became harder and harder to distract myself with my daily activities. It saddened me even more that no one noticed. Either that, or I was pretty good at hiding it. But I did perceive from family members that I was stupid. I got an F in spelling in Miss Vail's class, and that confirmed my stupidity. I was actually fine at school and thoroughly enjoyed being with Cheryl, but I couldn't escape how I felt at home. I felt worthless! The weeks dragged by and the feelings persisted. One evening, after the dishes were done, I snuck into the bathroom and decided that I had had enough of trying to cope with the melancholy. Going back to T.J. and O.C., whom I needed to be with more than anyone else in the world, wasn't happening. It would be an intolerable number of years before the opportunity to be with them again would come around. My parents, my brothers, and my sisters were all university educated (or would be soon), and I would never come anywhere close. I didn't want to feel worthless anymore. I thought, "My family may have wanted me to feel stupid, but I was not going to confront anyone about it. I simply felt alone."

There was a straight razor in the cheap little medicine cabinet in the bathroom, and I gathered the courage to just "do it". I envisioned letting the blood flow from the artery in my left wrist. I wanted to end my suffering. I made a precise cut. No blood. It wasn't as easy as I thought it would be. I took some deep breaths, and made another cut over the same spot. To my surprise, no blood came again; yet, I could see the blood pulsing through, so I knew I was in the right spot. I made a third cut, gingerly this time because it hurt and all of a sudden, I envisioned my blood squirting all over the place and making a huge mess. I put my hands on the sink and breathed deeply. I thought, "Holy cow. No blood. Maybe I'm not supposed to do this to myself. I have to go on living." I put a Band-Aid on the cut and no one noticed. This time I was benefitting from my policy of not sharing. There was no need to explain what I had just attempted. Silently, I gave myself a cheering speech: "I know that I am a trooper and I can tolerate this emotional pain. I will couch my grief in the comfort of the Lord. And I will tell no one." And that is exactly what I did; I told no one. Not until I met Rob and I shared everything with him did any other person know of that event when I was 11.

I survived the suicide attempt, and am so grateful that my 11-year-old self was able to make the decision to not give in to the pain. Although my silent suffering would cause many more tears, in the weeks that followed that bathroom visit, I felt empowered and capable. My silence was a shield that protected me from external harm, and my inner determination was the fire I needed to keep going.

Unfortunately, not everyone faced with similar emotional turmoil survives. If you, or anyone you know is dealing with depression, don't stay silent. Please, have the courage that I did not, and speak with someone about your sadness. When you share your feelings with someone else, it is amazing how much lighter you will feel. There is someone who wants to listen to your story and help lighten your load.

Curtain Calls

— *Alienation is not healthy. Do not shut yourself off from the world around you. Take the time to share your life with others, and you will benefit.*

— *If you need help, take advantage of the wonderful systems in place for crisis. You can call the national crisis hotline, or see if there is a local one in your city.*

— *General counseling services can be found almost everywhere, so don't be afraid to reach out for help. If you need specialized counseling, many options exist, such as grief counseling, or trauma therapy.*

— *When you notice yourself withdrawing due to sadness, allow your friends to help you through it. If that seems like a huge task, think of the person that YOU resonate with the best, and collaborate with him/her on your next steps.*

— *When someone tells you not to say a word under any circumstances, that's exactly when you do need to discuss the issue with trusted friends or professionals.*

CHAPTER 5

Sports Motivation

A few months after my suicide attempt, I went with a new girlfriend, Josie, to her Evangelical church. Josie lived on the mountain, and her church was on the mountain as well. When we went to the service on Saturday evening, I was blown away by the minister's message. Everything he said strongly resonated with my beliefs. It was as if God Himself planned my visit to the church that day. One of the songs that we sang during the service was, "This little light of mine. I'm going to let it shine. Let it shine, let it shine, let it shine!" I had been feeling weak and counting on the strength of Jesus silently for many years (since I was 6 years old) and just after I had almost given up was this evening of song. Towards the end of the service, the members of the congregation shared their love for Jesus; never had I felt so comfortable in a group of people. Then we sang, "Jesus loves me, this I know, for the Bible tells me so. Little ones to Him belong, they are weak, but He is strong. Yes, Jesus loves me. Yes, Jesus loves me. Yes, Jesus loves me, the Bible tells me so." After the sermon, we were invited to be "saved." I was so happy. I needed to be saved to increase my faith, and so I joyously gave my life to the Lord. That evening, all of a sudden, a lot was making sense to me. I felt independent and strong, like I could handle any adversity. I walked up to the front of the gathering and was saved and blessed, along with many others. It was a beautiful night, and it is a cherished memory.

The next few weeks were so peaceful. In my excitement, I shared my glorious "new" self with family members, which sadly fell flat. I realized that my faith was not something that I could share with my family because they viewed it as a fanatically religious point of view. It brought me back to being silent. I regretted not being able to share my happiness, but so be it: No one was going to stop me from feeling my newly found joy. I dreamt about the conflict in my dreams night after night. I learned a lot of lessons during this period of rejection, such as what to say and when to share. I did this so that I wouldn't impose my beliefs on others. Everyone is allowed to believe what he or she chooses. The gift of choice is one of the greatest gifts that we have ever been given. I was hugely at peace with myself. Whether I was accepted or rejected started to make no difference to me. Even though I knew I was different from others, with a dose or two (or three) of self-love, I was happy again.

Expanding

Cheryl and I were in Miss Davis's class in grade eight. She was a wonderful teacher and there was one thing that she said that still reverberates in my mind: "One in ten will be mentally ill in their life." For the longest time, I had no idea why this sentence popped into my head on occasion. When high school started, Cheryl and I started spending our time with different friends. At age 11, 12 and 13, I struggled with feeling inferior. I admitted to myself that I had an inferiority complex. When I realized that I was thinking negatively, I fought to think positively instead.

My world was expanding and so was I. I was gaining weight and feeling fat. Father often had drug-company representatives come by and leave newly approved drug samples. I knew he had some amphetamine weight loss samples, so I went to his apothecary and I took them, knowing that he would not notice. I read the label and the side effects, and thought I was in business.

For the next three months, I was on track. I was losing weight and had tons of energy; as a result, I started to join every athletic team for which I qualified. At this time, I was in grade 9 in a high school that had so many students that for one year, we had to go in two shifts: one from 7 a.m. to 1 p.m., and another from 2 p.m. to 7 p.m. I was in the morning shift, and many of my middle school classmates were no longer in my class. In fact, there was no one that I chummed with in any of my classes, and so I followed a nine-subject rotation system alone in my program. I already knew how to feel comfortable with being alone, so I was just following the beat of my own drum.

Athletics

During my high school years, I decided that since I couldn't compete with my siblings intellectually, I would excel in athletics, which is exactly what I did. In grades 9, 10, 11, and 12, I was on the interscholastic basketball and volleyball teams. We usually won against all the other high schools in the city, as evidenced in our high school yearbooks, which proudly showed our achievements. I also played badminton doubles once a week, and I loved playing on the team. We didn't reach city championship status in badminton, but that was okay—it was the pleasure of playing the sport that was important to me. I also went swimming every night for a few years in grades seven and eight, but when Jimmy Thompson, the coach, assessed my swimming, he said that I was like a potato in the water. He was blunt and truthful and I had no problem facing the reality that swimming was not suited for my physique.

As my teen years went by, instead of swimming in the pool, I started diving. There was no competition or coaching, I just enjoyed the sport a great deal. Most of the time, I was part of a team but this was one thing that I chose to do alone, in the pockets of my free time. I tried baseball but wasn't very good at it, which was also true with track and field. No matter how hard I tried, I was not a fast enough runner to be competitive. On the other hand, most of the summer camps that I went to had Ping-Pong tables, and I was very good at that. I've been told that when I was a child, my motor skills developed much faster than normal, which may explain my achievements in sports.

I received the Award of Merit for swimming at age 14, which was my highest earliest achievement. I also became a Red Cross swimming instructor at age 16, which is not often done. I didn't share this with my family because I didn't want to give them the opportunity to mock what had been an effort for me. Don't get me wrong, my brothers and sisters are wonderful people; however, due to my involuntary family shift exposures, I was more sensitive and vulnerable to comments that I construed as hurtful. It was my mindset, as well as the attitude of my family members, that contributed to this dynamic.

Growing Pains

My love of music is huge. From toddlerhood on, music has soothed my soul. When my girlfriends and I started going to dances every Friday, Saturday and Sunday, I was happy except when I was at home. This was my motivation to be out of the house as much as possible. I was grateful for any freedom away from the house. Once, when my favorite pink blouse was ripped off me in the basement when I was thirteen, my resolve for independence increased. And so, when I took a trip on my bike the next summer from 9 a.m. to 9 p.m. on a day when I wasn't at camp, and came home later than expected, I was undeterred. My mother had given me permission early in the morning to go on a daylong bike ride. As punishment for arriving hours later than expected, my parents ordered me to get on the examining table in the office. When they asked,

I told them that I had spent the day with friends in Winona. They said nothing other than that I had been disobedient. They pulled down my pants and took turns spanking my bare bum many times. What they didn't know was that I could feel their emotion and their energy. The three of us loved each other, but they had chosen to instill their discipline in a way with which I was completely out of sync. After they allowed me to stand up and pull up my pants, I had something to say in return.

Without malice, this is what I declared: "No matter how much you choose to punish me for whatever I do, I will not be stopped from doing it. I will go where I want, when I want, and return at my time of choosing." My parents both looked at me with frowns on their faces. They had nothing to say in return. The style of parenting that they were familiar with had not worked and they knew it. They also knew that up until that point, I had been a co-operative daughter, doing all that I could to comply with their rules. They knew that I was non- confrontational and that I was deeply religious; however, I was no longer accepting their style of parenting. They were totally capable of understanding where I was coming from as they had chosen not to support me in the face of adversity within the family. This was never discussed, not then and not in all the years thereafter.

Caregiving

Let me share something important with you at this point in my story. I became the main caregiver for my parents in their senior years, and I thank and appreciate my brothers and sisters for allowing me to be the one to accept that role. It was a labor of love. I felt like I was receiving more than I ever gave during those senior years when our bonding was greater than it had been in all the previous years. Gerontology and palliative care were my focus during my nursing career, inspired by my four parents. In spite of our differences during those early years, I dearly love my entire family.

Before I continue with my teen years, I want to tell you about a dinner that we had the day before Thanksgiving in 2014. My sister, my brother, Pieter, Pixie: Pieter's wife, our cousin Jacob, Rob and myself had a wonderful family dinner. Pieter, Pixie and Jacob approved of my giving their real names in this book, which I deeply appreciate. At that dinner, Pieter explained what had happened to him when he was out of the parental home for a year. His need to dismiss religious fervor was established that year.. One of the things that I really enjoyed was listening to the discussions that we had around the dinner table.

Also, Jacob, who lives in Holland and who is in touch with all of the extended family of our father, explained that Tante Thilde (whom I was named after: Mathilde) wrote several books that had a mercurial approach to time frames, and an overall creative writing style. That is exactly how I have always wanted to write, so from now on, I am going to take more liberties of going back and forth time-wise. It is interesting that a style of writing was passed on from one generation to the next, without either Tante Thilde or myself knowing each other's style. I have not been able to read her work because reading Dutch is too laborious, but my family has translated her stories for me. Jacob's sister has also written a couple of Dutch books, and on my mother's side, I have a second cousin who is a prolific author of a children's book series. I tell you all of this to support my belief that nothing is a coincidence. All is planned, even though we have a freedom of choice.

Gaining Independence

When I was fourteen, I was fully enjoying my high school experience, and decided that I wanted to try a cigarette. It was the popular thing to do. Soon, I was smoking my favorite brand, Alpine. The package had a mountain on it, and I especially liked the menthol taste. It wasn't until I met my future husband, Rob, eight years later that I succeeded in finally quitting this awful addiction.

In high school, I was earning weekly pocket money on my own, but I confess that I also took money that my mother saved for groceries from a fancy wooden box kept in a desk drawer. I took the money so I could buy what I wanted so badly—two or three new love comics or classics every week. I read and reread those love comics. They were a great comfort. I felt no guilt for stealing the money, and my mother thankfully never noticed. After the declaration when I was 14, I was enjoying my newfound confidence and the intensity of my emotions.

Adventures

Cheryl and I reunited our friendship later in high school, and we would take daylong treks going as far as we could on the railway tracks. We had fun by letting our imaginations run free, and daydreaming about our futures. Once or twice, on weekends, we decided to go up the steps at Wentworth and count them all on the way up. We would lose count and work all the harder to be accurate on the way down. There are something like 254 steps to reach the top of "the Mountain." Tittering and giggling was all part of the fun. We were starting to share with each other which boys we liked. Once, I went on my own in the parks and woods that were beyond the Hamilton Rock Gardens. I loved being free and exploring. I was grateful that I was independent and allowed to explore without fear.

For one year, I was in C.G.I.T., or Canadian Girls In Training. It was an organization that was similar to "Guides" with a bit more of a religious bent, but I didn't really like the other members. I stopped going after that year; however, the baton twirling and tap dancing are still good memories. Every weekend Cheryl and Sue and I went to a dance at St. Giles Presbyterian Church on Friday night, to Ryerson United Church on Saturday night, and when we were older, to the Germania Club on Sunday nights. I loved dancing and I was good at it. These three nights of dances every weekend were what we lived for. A few months later,

I started going out with boys. These relationships were an exercise in socializing. At one point I had three boyfriends whose first names were all "Jim!" I remember my mother's sister saying, "You've got your boyfriends all having the same name to make it easy for yourself!" I laughed and saw the truth of it.

Discovering sexual attraction was exciting and I was all for looking for the "right guy." One boyfriend whom I really liked had introduced me to "French necking," and after that it was my new limit. I knew that there was "more" to do, and so I talked about it with my mother. She explained to me that boys at that age have uncontrollable hormones, which means that they often don't really care about the girls, they just want to sexually relieve themselves. I listened carefully and I agreed. From that point on, I was very careful.

Lessons

My mother also explained to me that no man looking for a wife (one who would honor the marriage covenant) would want soiled goods. When you enter the marriage chamber after the wedding, you need to be a virgin or you are "vies." "Vies" means dirty. When my mother used the word "vies," there was a lot of contempt behind it. Hearing that word from her mouth gave me the shivers; I hated hearing her say it. I never told her my aversion to that word, but I knew that I didn't want to be "vies."

My mother taught me many lessons in my early teens, and I listened carefully. She went to great lengths, using Greek mythology, to explain the different kinds of love:

1. Love for self
2. Platonic love (as a friend)
3. Love leading to intimacy
4. Love for mankind

All these loves are enhanced by the use of the mind. Our mind is the most precious organ/muscle that we can exercise to improve our life, our human experience. Remember that we have a soul that will not die when our body does; I am speaking now from the point of view of my experiences as a Palliative Care Registered Nurse. I was on the front lines of the death experience. Why I am including this here is because *birth*, *death* and *love* are all closely related in the mind. I feel these events very intensely because that is where my mind has been focused for decades. In these high school years, I came to a crossroads that led me on a straight path to where I am today. Looking back, I can see the straight path, but as a teenager this direction and what lay ahead for me were not so clear.

The lessons using Greek mythology were my favorite precious times with my mother. I "felt" her joy as she was relating what she had learned and what was important to her. I remember her telling me, "Loving someone is as much in the brain as it is in the body. When love is nurtured in the body, mind and soul, it is a fulfilling, beautiful experience." This truth that she told me came true. My husband Rob and I are blessed in our covenant union.

During my teen years, my brothers and sisters and parents taught me the joy of being in a family that was fully aware. Our pleasure was shared, issues were discussed, and our brains were well exercised to the extent that we all felt fully alive. Our need for philosophizing followed. How many families nurtured this level of thinking? We discussed the Second World War and Darwin's theory of the survival of the fittest. We discussed religion and spirituality, and this is where I learned that it was better to keep my mouth shut. My views were not accepted or appreciated. One has to navigate a social labyrinth before one can be fed at our van Vierssen Trip family table. The lessons that I was learning regarding the two families that I had been privileged to be a member of were invaluable in dealing with my later psychotic disorder. I am now not only mentally healthy and physically healthy, but I achieved that after being fully handicapped. Now I am blessed to share my tools of recovery with you.

Curtain Calls:

- *Be careful with the language that you use with others, especially when they are emotionally vulnerable. Your words may carry a powerful impact, good or bad, depending on your intended message.*
- *Kindness and generosity are much appreciated. Over time, you will see these two main traits returned to you ten fold, or even 100 fold.*
- *You can train your mind to go in the direction that you want it to go, so pick a healthy and beautiful destination.*
- *Let what I write prod you to giving your life history and your current circumstances some deep, introspective thought.*
- *No matter what happens to you, keep feelings of forgiveness at the forefront of your mind through difficult times, as they are a soother for your soul.*

CHAPTER 6

Amsterdam Crossroads

In 1964, at age nineteen, I moved back to Holland to start nursing school. Going back to Holland was what I had been praying for, over the years. Finally, I was home. Tante Jannie and Oom Cees welcomed me with open arms. We loved each other so very much and had missed each other more than we could each express. All was right in the world when I was in the presence of Tante Jannie and Oom Cees. We discussed whatever we liked and there was a huge sense of love that permeated our surroundings. Abundance, happiness and a sense of balance had come back into our lives.

Summer Fun

Within weeks of arriving, we went on a wonderful holiday to Austria with a couple who were close friends of the family. For the five of us to fit in one car, we had to carefully decide what to pack for the two weeks. The scenery and the mountain air were awesome, and our time together flew by. When we came back to Holland, I went on another holiday, this time camping for two weeks with Tante Jannie's sister, her husband, and my cousin Willie, their daughter. The campgrounds were deluged with rain during our first few days, but that didn't stop us. Willie and I had a lot of fun and adventure on the grounds, and we made wonderful memories.

A few weeks later, the summer was over and I had to leave to start my nursing courses in Amsterdam. My previous four summers had been entirely spent working in the tourism industry. The first summer, when I was fifteen, I had worked at the same resort where my sister was a waitress. I had washed dishes from morning until night for eight weeks. The next two summers, I had been a chambermaid, and the fourth summer, I worked behind the bar of a resort on Manitoulin Island, near where my parents lived. Spending this summer with T.J. and O.C. was a welcome and much needed time of relaxation and family bonding; I will always fondly remember those days.

The Wilhelmina Guesthouse

As much as I regretted leaving T.J. and O.C., I was excited about starting my new, independent life. I was one of over one hundred new nursing students at a large teaching hospital in Amsterdam, "Het Wilhelmina Gasthuis." Translated, this means: "The Wilhelmina Guesthouse." The hospital had over a 1000-bed capacity and was located in several separate buildings. It was guarded and gated; a watchman was present in a cubbyhole at the main entrance gate, 24/7. This made me feel very secure.

All of the nurses in training lived eight to a dorm-room. The ceilings were over 10 feet high and there was lots of space around each bed. We each had a good single bed and all the white wardrobe closets were along one wall. My previous fourteen camp experiences had me feeling right at home. Thirty-two student nurses were in my class. We also each earned 137.50 guilders every month, which I was especially happy about. This would keep me comfortably financially independent. Also, every single classmate was open and non judgmental. I could feel a positive energy in our class, and there were two friends that I resonated well with, right from the start. One of them was Tanya from Australia. I'm so sorry that we've lost touch over the years.

All our classes were in Dutch and I was working hard to assimilate all that I was learning. Finally, I was where I wanted to be and nothing stood in my way. We learned how to look after cut flowers from arrival to display in the correctly chosen vase. We learned how to improve our comfort level with patients on the various wards. This was a very gentle introduction to patient care. Our textbook classes were in the afternoons, after being on morning duty in the wards. It was fun and exciting.

Most weekends, I went to visit T.J. and O.C., but I was also making time to visit other relatives who lived nearby. These were relatives on my father and mother's side who I previously never got to see because when I was in Holland ten years earlier, I made the decision to leave out these two extended families. The extended families of Tante Jannie and Oom Cees were enough for me when I was 9-10. It was at my Grandmother's request that I came to visit. About once a month during that Amsterdam year, I visited my Grootmoeder. I could feel that she was missing her husband, my Grootvader, who had died a few years earlier. During my year in Amsterdam, I was not aware that she and Grootvader had paid for my return trip back to Holland when I was nine years old. I wish I had of thanked her for that gift.

My mother's older sister, Tante Adrie, and her husband, Oom P.J. Koets, were empty nesters living just one tram ride away. They were so very welcoming and glad to see me. Tante Adrie was trained as an M.D. but she never talked about medicine. Oom P.J. had been a Deputy Mayor of Amsterdam for a few years and before that, he had been the editor of "Het Parool," a major Dutch newspaper. But it wasn't their education that impressed me, it was their warmth and sharing of love that I soaked up when we were together. Tante Adrie is whom I was named after: Adriana.

An Unexpected Visit

About five weeks into the nursing program, I was requested to go to the nursing office, but I had no idea why I was called. A friend of my father, Dr. van Biema, was waiting to see me. He had come from Apeldoorn, where T.J. and O.C. lived, but they did not know each other. Dr. van Biema took me to a small receiving lounge and talked with me in earnest. His mission was to convince me that I was making a mistake. He was representing my father, and, knowing the current Dutch health care system better than my father, he knew what was best for me. It was in early October 1964, and I was nineteen. He told me, "Maar lieve kind, je hoort hier niet." Translated, he had said, "But dear child, you don't belong here." That sentence was branded into my brain because I listened, did what was advised, and yet the decision to leave ended up being the wrong one.

His advice was sincerely given; he was Jewish, had survived the war, and I respected and trusted his judgment. I didn't see him again after that day, though. In order to follow his advice, I had to leave fast. I have never been able to see into the future, and this wasn't the only wrong decision that I have made. On the other hand, since I still have no doubt that this was the direction in which I was meant to go, it was ultimately a good decision in the long run.

The next day, I went to "The Directrice." She was the Director of Nursing for the hospital and she was a very kind, approachable lady. I requested a transfer to the hospital that Dr. van Biema had encouraged me to go to: "De Prinsengracht." This was a hospital where ladies of refinement trained, and the first thing I noticed was that my monthly pay was reduced to half of what I had previously been making. However, my hospital change had been made, and I was committed to all that was to come. I felt like I was meant to make this change, but I didn't know why. I had my Bible and sought comfort in its verses.

I said goodbye to my newfound friends and they looked as confused about my decision as I felt. I realized that I hadn't consulted T.J. and O.C., but I thought that their advice would not be relevant to making an accurate assessment of my choices. When I have a hard time with a choice, I pray alone and I follow what I am "led" to do. This is something that I am sharing with you now even though it takes me out of my comfort zone, because I know there will be people who read this and judge me for feeling "led." Keep in mind that in this book, I am offering hope, inspiration and motivation: These are spiritual feelings. I cannot offer these spiritual feelings without being completely honest about where I am coming from. What you take from reading my story is a choice that you are allowed to make, but I encourage you at this time to practice being non-judgmental. This is how we will all create more love for each other.

The Prinsengracht

The Prinsengracht Hospital was a place that I was led to experience. It was a smaller, non-teaching hospital where the atmosphere was completely different from where I had just come. Everyone was just as friendly and kind, but among the students I felt a sense of "competition" that was not a part of my philosophy. I felt a strong sense of judgment and that produced an uncomfortable vigilance in me. I was nineteen years old and was well aware of what I liked and didn't like. Within days, I knew I had made a mistake. It was correct for me to have listened to Dr. van Biema though, so I gave it some more thought. I started to think about my situation in regards to following the path of the Lord. However, there wasn't anyone there with whom to share such thinking, and I felt lonely. As a result, I was even more eager to go by tram each weekend to the train station, so that I could spend every possible minute with T.J. and O.C. We didn't talk often about religion or spirituality; it was just understood.

After that first weekend at home, I went to the market in Amsterdam and bought myself a variety of different colored gourds. I put them on display in a bowl on a little table in the middle of the room, and I sat cross-legged on the floor, admiring the gourds and enjoying my single room with gratitude. I realized that some depression was settling in, but suicidal thinking had been on the back burner for years, so I wasn't worried about the thoughts resurfacing.

A few weekends before Christmas, a cousin of my father's had invited me to her house because she had some items for my room. My private room was quite nice and was enhanced with my own "things." My father's cousin, Tante Toos Massee, was a wonderful, kind, generous lady who greeted me like we had known each other forever. The bond was immediate. She had several children who were no longer living at home. Her beautiful home was sumptuously appointed. She gave me a hand-made, room-sized Turkish carpet, several small, carved wood tables, several beautiful lamps and more. I accepted all this abundance with great gratitude. I marveled at her generosity and I could feel that our love was mutual, despite this being our initial meeting. After her visit, my private room at The Prinsengracht was beautiful.

Even though I was thrilled to connect with my cousin, my desire to be with T.J. and O.C. for every possible moment was overwhelming. I was homesick. Even though I was in Holland, I still had a feeling of not being with T.J. and O.C. to the extent that I needed. I had visited Tante Wout van Iterson on the "Gold Coast" of Amsterdam several times. Twice I went to her house in the suburbs, and twice she met me downtown near the Hospital. She was the fiancé of my father's brother who had committed suicide a few decades earlier. We never once mentioned that tragedy, but there was a lot that was silently understood. She stayed in touch with our family for the rest of her life. I liked her and I regretted that she had lost my soft-spoken uncle. She never married and never had children. It felt like I was her niece, and family was important to her, which made me feel loved. She was a scientist and I respected her a lot. She was also someone from whom I felt no judgment; she accepted me exactly as I was.

One of my first tasks at the Prinsengracht was washing dishes alone by hand; a lot of them. That day there were about five girls sitting on the counter watching me and grilling me. I remember thinking to myself that one summer of washing dishes when I was fifteen was enough for me. I felt as if this experience was meant to put me in my place. Each new student had to do this task as an initiation. It was abhorrent to me. In the weeks that followed, my evenings were spent alone in my room; I was alienating myself again like I had years before. I spent my free time listening to the three large 78" RPM vinyl records that I owned. Sadly, there was no money to buy more. I was not going to ask my parents or T.J. and O.C. for money. I needed to stay financially independent. Although I knew that I was depressed, I still had no noticeable thoughts of suicide.

The training program was three years long, with approximately eighteen students in each class. There was camaraderie while we were on the wards in uniform. We were taught how to use five big feather pillows to make someone really comfortable in bed. I used that skill many times in the future, and am very glad to have learned it. We had one teacher who was really special. Her name was Zuster Marrianne Wolters. Zuster means sister. She was single and from Apeldoorn, my hometown. Rob (my husband) and I reconnected with her in 2007 and she remembered who I was. She also knew my parents and we enjoyed seeing each other again. She was a beloved teacher of many. Even with her as a guide, my depression did not lift and over the months, my self- imposed oppression increased.

The Crossroads

More and more I realized that I was at a crossroads. My focus on the Dutch studies was difficult. My integration back into Dutch society didn't "feel" right. I wasn't studying enough and, at the end of the year, I failed the exams. When I was with T.J. and O.C., as much as we loved each other, I still didn't feel integrated. It was the Dutch society and culture with which I was not resonating enough. In the early summer of 1965, my mother was in Holland for a visit and I told her that all I could see every day were the grey skies. I was missing the Canadian climate with the many blue-sky days. I was missing the convenience and culture of Canada.

The telephone was used more often in those years than the years before, and I had a girlfriend from the other hospital that wanted to go to Paris with me for five days before I went back to Canada. Yes, the decision to go back to Canada was made. My crossroads was over. When I told T.J. and O.C. of the decision, I felt their disappointment. These were big ties that I was cutting. They were truly "losing" me for a second time. That's why I called my love for them addictive. I was unable to function as a member of society; my need for them was so great. I wasn't meant to become dependent again on them; that time had passed. It would be six years before I would see them again, and the love between us was there as much as ever, but so was the pain. It went unsaid, like so much else in our family.

That same summer when I was twenty, Tante Jannie's, her sister, her husband, Oom Cees and I went on a car trip to Austria. We visited old haunts like "Heiligen Blut", or "Holy Blood," a charming little town, high in the mountains. After that, my girlfriend and I went to Paris by train for five glorious days and there was an added exciting adventure that I will include in a later book. We came home happy and healthy, with lots of wonderful memories.

The Amsterdam Crossroads were when my future was decided. The question was: "Stay in Holland, or go back to Canada?" After a lot of thought, I was confident that my decision was the right one. Just like T.J. and O.C. had taught me not to complain about the turn of events, they didn't complain or try to dissuade me from my course of action. All around me, I felt support, and in that, I felt love. Mentally, I was happy that my destiny was taking me to where my father had made a similar decision a generation earlier. My nursing career would be in Canada where the society was more my style. I had grown accustomed to Canada, after all.

Lessons Learned

That year, I realized more than ever that we are each following a destiny. Even though we have the freedom of choice, the closer we pay attention to where we are "led," the greater our human potential will be. At this time, I knew about Herbert W. Armstrong, a great 20th century humanitarian, who wrote the book, *The Incredible Human Potential* thirteen years later. The Philadelphia Church of God has this book available on request. At the time, this book was not yet a guiding light for me. But I knew of "The World Tomorrow" and "The Plain Truth" monthly literature pamphlets that were related to this, and these also led me back to Canada.

The awareness of my duality gave me food for thought. My depression lifted with the prospect of a new beginning in Canada. I had given reintegrating into Dutch society a full year with the realization that growing up with Tante Jannie and Oom Cees was an image never to be fulfilled. Whether this fed into my depression that would worsen over the next decades, I don't know. Any one thing does not cause depression. For someone to tell you to just snap out of it shows his/her misunderstanding. Training the mind takes a conscious effort that is very, very difficult, especially when the mind is injured or weak. Saying goodbye to Tante Jannie and Oom Cees was difficult this time because I was leaving due to a decision that I was solely responsible for. It was so hard to forgive myself for the pain that I was inflicting on them, but I did. I knew that I had to live my life for my sake, not theirs.

This period of my life was filled with many new, exciting experiences, and many difficult learning lessons. I matured as a young woman, and started making big life decisions on my own. I had the opportunity to a life in Holland as I had dreamed of for so many years, only to realize that I preferred the Canadian culture and lifestyle. Overall, I learned to trust my instincts, and listen to the calling of the Lord.

Curtain Calls

- *The Universe is your friend. Allow this friend to give you comfort.*
- *The more in tune you are with your feelings, the more likely it is that you are going in the right direction.*
- *Before making life-changing decisions, boost your confidence in yourself. Look at all the options before taking action.*
- *Give yourself a chance. Trust in yourself. If you believe in God, nurture a trust in yourself and God.*
- *Whatever happens, forgive yourself and others if things don't turn out the way you thought they would. Nurture strength of spirit.*
- *In previous generations the feeling of blame was rampant. I would love to see blame, judgment, and non-forgiveness disappear from our social consciousness.*

CHAPTER 7

The Ryerson Years

It was August 1965, and I was twenty years old on the voyage back to Canada. There was no more wishing and praying about going to Holland. This closed chapter was a regret that brought back my thoughts of suicide. These thoughts resulted from my rootless feelings, and were suppressed as I realized that this type of thinking came in waves. Just like the waves on the ocean, sometimes the seas were relatively calm and sometimes the waves were huge and the water was choppy. Looking at the waves echoed my emotional insecurities. A balancer on the ship prevented it from listing, which made it a better, more enjoyable trip for everyone on board. Likewise, I resolved not to let my emotions get the better of me and cause me to focus on the negative.

Once on land, I immediately sought the refuge of my parents. They had not changed and that gave me some comfort. My parents were paying for my next three years at Ryerson, which I deeply appreciated. The few weeks before school were spent roaming around Manitoulin Island. My parents lived in a house that they had expanded, in the town of Manitowaning. The house that my parents lived in was well furnished. There were some very big, luscious plants on the foyer level that one walked by from the kitchen to the large 24-foot by 16-foot living room. They had finally purchased a big color T.V. I felt the abundance again, which gave me a richness that I soaked up.

Manitoulin Island

Manitoulin Island is the largest fresh water island in the world. The geography of rock and fauna formations is unique; as a result, the island gave me a feeling of bonding with spirit. I could understand how the natives felt "close" to the land. Manitoulin Island has a marine climate because there is water all around. Feeling the raw nature and wide expanses soothed my soul. The name "Manitou" is "God" and "waning" is "home." I did indeed feel like I was at home.

My father's mother "Grootmoeder," visited for a few weeks that summer. My sister also visited, and my brother's wife with her three daughters (my nieces), were there too. It was a full house, and enjoying the family brought its rewards. At one point during the visit, someone spoke harsh words about me, and as a result, I went, to a little house (on our property) that had no bathroom and no heat and I hid there for hours. I felt confused, and angry with myself for being so sensitive to what others in the family said. I realized that it was up to me to take a different perspective and that in turn, I would become a stronger person.

Being different was part of who I was, and I told myself that it was time that I accepted and loved myself for who I was, instead of feeling bad about whom I wasn't. It was okay for me to think differently because my opinion mattered. In this beautiful land where I felt so connected to myself, I realized that suicidal thoughts would pop into my head regularly, but that I could deny myself that thought process. In other words, as soon as a suicidal thought came up, I would consider it not "my" thinking. I had control over what type of thinking I allowed. I had the power to make the conversation in my mind go in the direction that I wanted.

Support System

That was the summer that I first met Robert and Bernadette; he was a teacher and she worked as a nurse for my father at "The Clinic." They were a wonderful couple who were very aware and full of life. They enriched the lives of all the people they met and I saw them as role models. They were in Canada for just a few years, after which they would return to their native home of Northern Ireland. In the meantime, we spent a lot of joyous hours together. Robert has now passed away, but I still exchange Christmas cards with Bernadette every year. The reason why I am sharing this is to illustrate that it is good to nurture relationships. When you meet someone with whom you resonate, encourage a closer relationship with that person. It is not possible to have too many friends. When you have developed a lot of close friends by "doing unto them" what you would like "them to do unto you," you've developed a strong support system.

In this way, there is nothing wrong with being more of a giver than a receiver; it means that you can nurture your strength of spirit. Give to those who are open to receiving what you have, and you will develop a stronger sense of intuition. Bernadette is an excellent example of this principle. I now realize that what I saw in her was the gift of comfort that she gave to people when anyone was in her presence. If you know what I'm describing, then you have met such people yourself.

After this eventful and fun summer, I felt confident about my future. My parents drove me to Toronto to find an apartment. We found a lovely single-bed sitting room in an old home not far from public transportation at Yonge and St. Clair. It was a 30-minute walk and subway ride from my room to Ryerson Polytechnic Institute, and I was ready for the adventure. At my new school, the nursing program was totally geared to learning. There was no menial work required to offset the cost of the education like in Holland. This was a forward thinking program for nursing, even by Canadian standards. I had chosen this over being at a teaching hospital in Toronto or Hamilton because I felt that my time would be more effectively used, and I was very grateful that my parents supported me financially.

For a long time after moving to Canada my mother did not learn how to drive, but I gave this dependence on my father no consideration. We didn't ever discuss it, and to my surprise, my mother got her driver's license a few years after I returned to Canada for nursing school. My mother didn't really share her struggles with me. In hindsight, I would have liked her philosophizing to have included her personal struggles. She may not have shared her personal struggles for the same reason that I did not share my suicidal thinking. Speaking these thoughts out loud or writing them down puts them out into the universe, and makes the struggle all the harder to manage.

Ryerson

At Ryerson, it was invigorating to be in a class where everyone came with the same set of advantages. I loved not having to struggle with a language barrier. I made several good friendships, and all was right in my world. We had good teachers and the program was just two or three years old. Later in the year, we had an assembly where we were told that our three years of courses would count towards getting a Bachelor's degree in Nursing. This gave me a sense of awe. My siblings would never believe that I was capable of completing such a thing. It was a dream come true!

Even though it had been years since I had done any springboard diving, there was a lovely pool on campus where I tried my old skill. When I saw my picture in the Ryerson newspaper the next week, I felt a bit embarrassed. It didn't make sense for me to have felt badly because it was a good picture of me in the middle of a well-executed dive; why was I feeling so shy? I realized that it was in part because no one had seen the picture, and thus there was no support or comment on my venture. Conversely, I wanted to stay anonymous because even though I thought I was able to take whatever came my way in stride, it wasn't the reality for me at all. This event showed me that I was actually off base emotionally. I was back to feeling different from others, and wanting to alienate myself and stay quiet.

Learning About Trust

On a warm, late fall evening, I gathered the nerve to go to a dance alone. It was a lovely walk there and I felt happy and excited about the night ahead. I would integrate myself on the dance floor. This was where I had shone in the past, and I wanted to recapture that feeling. Listening to the music while floating in a man's arms had always boosted my mood, and I was looking forward to a positive experience this time around. After I arrived, several men asked me to dance. I knew that men liked dancing with good partners. There was one man who was especially appealing to me. It was his warmth and style that I liked. He was charming and gave me a feeling of joy and ease. We danced every classical dance together and at the evening's end, he invited me to his room. He explained that he had a nice place just a 30-minute walk away, and he promised he would take good care of me. He was gentle and kind with his offer and since I was enjoying myself, I said yes.

I trusted him and we had a leisurely walk to his rooming house, chatting all the way. When we got to his room, he showed me some games using dice and cards. We were both sitting cross-legged on the floor and I was very comfortable with him. After about thirty or forty minutes, I decided that it was late and time for me to go home. We agreed to see each other at the next dance event, and I put my coat on and had my hand was on the doorknob when he jumped up and grabbed me! At lightening speed, he tore off my coat, and tried to unbalance me. I started to struggle and he warned me to stay quiet. He whispered into my ear that if I screamed or yelled, I would be in deep trouble. His manner and tone frightened me. There was no time for me to think as I struggled to get away. However, my attempts to escape didn't stop his aggression. There was no kissing; he used his strength to throw me onto his bed without my consent.

He had a double bed that took up most of the square footage of the room. His thin, dirty old mauve bedspread was bunching up under me and I was briefly conscious of it hampering my efforts to get away. My legs were bigger and stronger than his, my weight about the same, with him being several inches taller. Silently, I was confident that I would succeed in getting him off me because I was athletic and strong. I asked him to stop and told him that I was a virgin. But he kept going. After a few minutes, I knew that I was in deep trouble. This was very much an assault and I told him to stop again. But he didn't and I felt panicked.

While we silently fought, he kept overpowering me. I was wearing a girdle and I was confident that he would not succeed in lowering it. I consciously stopped panicking and focused my attention on the moment. Time was going in slow motion. It dawned on me that he was enjoying this, and it made me feel nauseated and disgusted. He was relentless in his fight to make me succumb, and he was gaining. He managed to forcefully pull down my girdle despite my struggles. He pushed my legs apart by digging the fingers of one hand into my thigh while using the other hand to pin my arms above my head. He breached my defenses and made just enough room to penetrate me—I remember, it was painful!

I thought to myself, "Why does he keep going? Does he get a kick out of forcing me against my will?" He kept at it and I was like a rag doll because at that point I was exhausted. I don't know if I lost consciousness or just fell asleep. A little after six in the morning, I woke up to light coming through the curtain-less windows. I looked over and saw the sleeping aggressor. I quietly and gently lifted myself up off the old double mattress. I pulled up my pants and girdle and put on my coat. As I gingerly took each step, the floor creaked, but he didn't stir. The door was open and I escaped out of the room into a dark loft. I carefully walked down the stairs and quickly exited the house. The 30-minute walk home was a blur, but I could feel a cool breeze against my face that was soothing to my soul. Breathing air that smelled of fallen leaves gave me a sense of healing.

When I arrived at my room, I climbed into my comfortable single bed. I then burst into tears as a gamut of emotions quickly raced through my mind. I felt ashamed, blaming myself for what had just happened to me. How could I have been so stupid as to trust a stranger? Why had my judgment of this man been so mistaken? I realized the man must have been a pervert and I felt angry. What man does not listen to a woman when she says "No?" I felt very much alone with my thoughts on the ordeal. I wanted to crawl into a hole and die. Then I realized that I was desperate to undo the damage. I went to my well-equipped sewing basket, took out a big curved needle (used for sewing material onto furniture), held it over a flame, let the needle cool, propped up a mirror between my legs, and tried to sew my hymen back into place. It was awkward and painful. It wasn't working and I had to give up. I realized that someone might consider me a pervert if they knew what I was trying to do.

There was no way I could go to the hospital to report the rape. Who would believe me when I was foolish enough to willingly go to his room? There had been no alcohol. Being drunk was not a part of this event, however sometimes I wished it were. Maybe then I could remove some part of the memory. But for many, many months it remained crystal clear, cutting through my mind like a sharp knife.

I never went dancing again. When I went to class the next day, I could feel my face blushing. I was sore at my base and couldn't walk properly because of it. I felt like everyone could see the shame emblazoned on my face. I thought others knew that I was changed; that a man had had his "way" with me. My comfort with my colleagues in the class was gone. I told no one. No one in my class ever found out what had happened.

For the rest of that first year, I was like a robot. I remember one teacher saying to me that " I could not see the forest for the trees," and I couldn't figure out what she meant. I knew that it was a key, but I asked no one because my self-confidence was at an all time low. Suicidal thinking was something that came daily, but I still had control over it so that was not of immediate concern. When the summer came, I worked at a resort near my parents' home. The owners, a young couple, were very warm and understanding of their employees. They were also very relaxed, and this rubbed off on me. Also, the comfort of basking in the love and friendship of Robert and Bernadette was a relief. I understood that there were many people, not just a few, whom I could feel completely comfortable with. Cheryl and I reconnected that summer, which was very exciting. She came to Manitoulin Island and stayed with us for a few weeks before we went back to my room on Rosehill Ave.; my bed- sitting room was more than big enough for both of us.

Forever Friends

Cheryl was then a public school teacher and her bubbly personality had me picture myself as a happy student in her classroom. Count yourself fortunate when you have found a best friend. My self- confidence rose exponentially. We started dating men and we had fun. Feeling self-conscious was in the past, and boy was I grateful. Cheryl had a friend who wanted to live with us for the next year so we went to a model apartment nearby that caught our eye. If we rented a one- bedroom apartment and signed a lease for a year dividing the monthly cost into three, we could afford it. We signed the lease and it was done. Our apartment was on the southwest corner of the eighteenth floor of a 31-story high-rise. It was a new building and we were the first occupants of the apartment. We had a balcony facing west that overlooked a rooftop outdoor swimming pool that was on the ninth floor. The high-rise was just a few steps away from the rear entrance to the Yonge and St. Clair subway stop. Cheryl, Margaret and I pitched in on the furniture and supplies that we needed and we were ready for an exciting year. Our three single beds filled the one bedroom and the rest of the apartment was made cozy, which made us very content.

It is with this backdrop that the stage was set for meeting Rob, my future husband. By that fall, I had been dating men for a year since that nightmarish event two years earlier. The men that I agreed to date were screened and I was getting pickier. I was actively looking for "the one and only." Rob and I met on November 4th, 1967. We asked our friend Ludo to come to a party that we were giving, and he asked if he could bring two friends from his boarding house. We said yes and that made for about twenty coming to the party with an equal number of men to women.

Soul mates

What a pleasant surprise this party would present. The chairs were around the walls, the table was against a wall, and we had a three-seat couch. There was enough seating for all twenty to sit, which dictated our invitation limit. I was immediately drawn to Rob who was sitting on a chair next to the doorway to the kitchen. He was fidgeting with his watch on his left wrist. There is such a thing as "love at first sight" because that is what happened to me. He was shy and he emanated his discomfort, which drew me in. Here was someone who would understand how I often felt.

I asked Rob about his watch and within minutes I asked him if he would like to talk with me in a more private place—the stairwell next to the rooftop. For the next few hours we talked and talked. He had an innocence that was appealing. My comfort level was great and both of us were reluctant to end the evening. When we said good-bye, neither of spoke about when we would meet again, but we both knew there would be a "next time". It was a night to remember!

From the very beginning, the connection between Rob and myself was powerful and sweet and pure. We had so much in common. For example, we had both immigrated to Canada at about the same age. He came to Canada from Bath, England, when he was five years old. The "Law of Attraction" was immediate—it was so easy to open up to Rob. What I felt was "no judgment" and he made it clear that he was enjoying my attention as well. I felt his attraction, but I also felt his respect and shyness, and it was manna to my soul. We fell asleep in each other's arms that first night and he didn't once try to kiss me, which I truly appreciated. Maybe I wasn't innocent anymore because of what had happened to me, but I knew that Rob was innocent and I loved it. What a relief, to have finally found my soul mate. The weekend went by in a happy haze and when I came home from school on Monday, a dozen yellow roses were delivered to our door. They were from Rob and I could hardly contain my happiness. Actions speak louder than words, and Rob's actions spoke volumes!

That was the beginning of our courtship, and we were inseparable. Within weeks, I told him about my rape experience and he understood my emotional pain. With Rob, I was able to come to terms with the event, as it was no longer important in the larger scheme of things. Rob was feeling swamped by his studies at the University of Toronto, he was getting his Masters of Science in Statistics, and I encouraged him to stay focused and get it done. We both started studying together and stayed on track. In early December, we both realized where our relationship was heading and we agreed to be married sometime in the next year, after we graduated. He invited me to meet his parents and his younger brother in Ottawa for Christmas and for the first time, I felt nervous. We had declared our love for each other, but I wasn't at all confident about Rob's family accepting me.

We drove to Ottawa from Toronto just before Christmas. Rob's Mom made me feel right at home and welcomed me to the family. She showed me the nicely decorated guest bedroom that I would be sleeping in, and put great effort into being a wonderful hostess. Rob's Dad, on the other hand, was terse with me. Rob told me after Christmas that his Dad had a man-to-man talk with him because he could see that Rob was serious about me. The experience of participating in my first Dunn family Christmas celebration was pure joy, clouded only by Rob's Dad's hesitancy towards our relationship. On our way back to Toronto, Rob and I went over the past few days and Rob gave me more details about his family's reactions. Rob also told me that his commitment to me had not changed. We both knew what we wanted and where we were going in life.

Rob knew about my tendency towards suicidal thinking, and he knew about my great passions and my strong emotions. I was so grateful and happy that he accepted and loved me for who I was. To this day, he is my soul mate and my best friend and I am forever grateful for him. I know that our life together has not been easy for him, but again, what doesn't break us makes us spiritually stronger. Our political views and religious views are pretty well matched, and we give each other room for a difference of opinion. The year we met was a year when my suicidal thoughts were virtually gone, and for that I was so grateful. Little did I know that this thinking would come back with a vengeance just two years later.

Rob and I studied mostly in his room in Toronto because there was more privacy than at my apartment. We had both done our best with buckling down and at the end of the year, we said good-bye to our friends and went to Ottawa for the summer. I was hired as a graduate at The Riverside Hospital in Ottawa and once I passed my Registration exams, I was promoted to Registered Nurse. Rob was rehired by Statistics Canada as a Statistician.

We set the date for our wedding as September 21st, 1968 at Kingsway United Church in Ottawa. Reverend Laverty, a professor at Queens' University, would officiate. I knew him from his summertime services on Manitoulin Island, and he was a friend of my parents. Rob and I looked at many model homes while he was living with his parents for the summer, and I rented an apartment with my sister. We decided on a house on South Park Drive in Blackburn Hamlet, just East of Ottawa. The house would be ready for us to move into right after the wedding. It was a summer of work and anticipation.

This period of my life contained significant highs and lows, the most important of which was my relationship with Rob. It was after meeting him that I knew that all the events in my life happened for a reason—they led me to him. Everyday I thank God for bringing Rob into my life. The events of this period taught me that when we experience terrible things, we can't give up because eventually life will get better and we will see the beauty all around us.

Curtain Calls

- *There are many people who have a huge strength of spirit. When time is spent in the company of these people, their great awareness may increase your sense of joy.*
- *When you are feeling "different" from others, avoid alienating yourself, Keep looking for those people who think positively and who will gladly accept your company. The search is worth the effort.*
- *You can train your mind. You have continuous choices to think one-way or the other. I recommend my friend Peggy McColl's book, "Your Destiny Switch", to help you get started on training your mind.*

— *Meditation is becoming more and more popular for a reason: it works. It means that you give yourself the time to understand what and why something has happened to you. By meditating, you are following through on loving yourself.*
— *Life throws curveballs. Self-pity does not serve you well. After your meditations, get into a wholesome, active discipline routine.*

CHAPTER 8

Marriage

With our marriage fast approaching, we decided to cover the costs ourselves so that we would have the freedom to choose what was important to us; as a result, the planning and preparations were a glorious gift. Rob and I were on a big, fat, fluffy cloud, and no one was allowed to burst our bubble. My sister was my Maid of Honor and the two oldest daughters of Pieter's were our flower girls. Rob's brother, Julian, was his Best Man and two of his friends were ushers. After all the invitations came back, we had a reception guest list of seventy-six guests, including both friends and family. Everything looked perfect.

It was painful for me that Tante Jannie and Oom Cees could not share what would be such an important experience in my life. Early in the summer, a big surprise package arrived and when I opened it, I cried quiet tears. In the package was a beautiful, heavy, white satin floor length gown with 4" wide white daisy appliques. The wedding dress fit me to perfection. Tante Jannie had not seen me for three years, and while we had sent few pictures, I was amazed that she knew my exact size. The dress was gorgeous. It had a crinoline and a ten foot-long delicate veil. There was also a shoulder length veil separately attached that would be lifted from my face during the ceremony. The package held matching white low-heeled shoes, which also fit perfectly, a little matching satin clutch bag on a chain, and elbow length white gloves. Tante Jannie knew I would love every single detail and design, and in this way, she and Oom Cees were part of the day after all.

We had picked "The Blue Note," which was a motel with a large dining room in Ottawa, as our reception venue and we were excited to have a live three-piece band with a D.J. Most of the people who were important to us would be there, our friends and my five older brothers and sisters and their families. Both Rob's and my parents were there, but with no extended families because they were in Europe. We had chosen an Ottawa photographer as well.

At least once a week, we drove to the building that was rising before our eyes—our new home. Now it is part of the Blackburn Hamlet suburb, but back then the neighborhood was just mushrooming into existence. The evening before our wedding, Sept. 20th, my three best girlfriends and I were able to sleep in our new house; this was where they helped me dress the following morning. We had a friend with an old model Oldsmobile who drove me to the church and then he drove both of us to the Blue Note.

On September 21st, 1968, when my father took me down the aisle, I was feeling nervous. I got cold feet. There was a lump in my throat and Rob looked very serious. These strong nerves of mine were ignored and I could hear myself choking as we said our vows. It was momentous! When I looked at Rev. Laverty's kind face and felt his gentle manner, my jangled nerves were calmed. The enormity of this moment was etched in my memory and I was glad of it, but the nervousness was something unpleasant that I had not expected. There was no doubt I wanted to marry Rob, and I felt happy, but also anxious. I know now that it was because I was experiencing my first real episode of what would later be called "a chemical imbalance."

The reception was etched into my memory as well. We have a photograph of my friends looking at "the ring" on my hand with the

Blue Note outdoor pool in the background. Once we were all seated at the long head table, little Earla (my 3 year old niece) came running up to the table in front of me with glee. She was spell bound by the Bride! Her mom, Gwen, quickly picked her high up into her arms and, with the two cuddling each other, took her back to their table. I felt a joy that I wished at that moment would last forever. In my heart, Rob and I were the most important people at that event, and our dinner was a gift that filled me with a generosity that would spread far and wide.

Just after we had seated ourselves, after Rob's welcoming toast, my mother came to me with a small-framed black and white photograph. It was a well-known picture of myself at four years old, sitting on T.J. and O.C.'s lap. I hadn't seen that picture in years. Tears of pain came to my eyes, but I choked them back. No one needed to see my sudden grief because they would not understand the extent of my emotional pain. I succeeded in controlling my visible emotions and gave this gesture of my mother's some thought. I realized that she had intended this gift to give me comfort. That it resulted in the opposite was something she didn't need to discover. It was her kindness that was important to me.

What a wonderful wedding and night to remember. The band was great, there was lots of dancing, and the D.J. was totally worth the cost. Time went by really fast, and before we knew it the night was over. Rob and I said goodnight to everyone and snuck off to our complimentary room on the second floor. Getting undressed, I felt a little nervousness again, but I quashed it. I remember removing the nylons from my legs and Rob lying in bed already with the covers up. I chuckled and joined him. The rest is predictable; I'll leave it to your imagination. The next day Rob and I went to the Dunn family cottage for two days, our first short honeymoon. We went swimming naked in the lake and promptly got a cold, but we both still went to work the next day.

We were feeling on top of the world. We had good jobs, we implemented our house and garden plans, and we had a sense of purpose in our action packed lives. That Christmas was the second consecutive one with the Dunn family, and I was feeling completely comfortable this time. We had the tradition of numbering all the neatly lined presents on the floor from where they came under the Christmas tree. The consecutive numbers on little slips of paper were placed in a hat, and with one number pulled out at a time, we opened our presents. This tradition continued once Rob and I started having our own children.

In the middle of the night that following April, around three a.m., Rob and I were woken by a phone call. It was my father telling me that mother had not eaten in five days, had not taken fluids in two, and that my coming to Manitowaning was urgent. I asked Rob to please contact my workplace immediately so that the staff could call in a replacement for me on my shift that was to begin at 7:15 a.m. Also, I asked Rob to tell them that I needed an indefinite leave of absence because I did not know how long my mother would need my care.

I was packed and on the road within the hour. Twice on the 500-mile trip, I tanked up and went to the bathroom, the rest of the time it was a marathon drive. I went past North Bay, Sudbury, Espanola and then Little Current. The Trans Canada Highway, (then called Highway 17), went right through all the centers of these towns in those days, so the monotony of the driving was broken up.

I arrived at my parents' home about 3 p.m. My father was sitting slumped in his favorite large, knobby grey chair. He didn't get up and I assumed that he was exhausted. As I walked through the house, I noticed that on every possible surface, items that had previously been stored in cupboards had now been placed on tables, counters and even the floor. I made a beeline to my mother who was lying languishing in their queen-sized bed. She didn't stir or smile when I came in and I sat on the bed beside her.

I quietly greeted her and with all the caring that I felt in my voice, I asked her if she could hear me. She made a tiny nod and I asked her if she could speak. In a weak voice, she slowly told me that she was very tired. She would not go back to the Sudbury Hospital, or any other hospital. She had been diagnosed with ulcerative colitis; eating was painful and made her sick. So far, it seemed that she was preparing for her death. I asked her if she would let me make her a cup of her favorite tea (no milk, 2 teaspoons of sugar). She said, "yes."

The stairs from the second floor to the kitchen were wide and grand with 5 steps, a large landing, and then 7 or 8 more steps. The ceilings in the old house were high because this was one of the grandest houses in town. Every surface was jam-packed. I ignored it and made the tea. My mother couldn't sit up to drink it. Luckily, she always kept straws in stock. I ran back downstairs and found them tucked away on a top shelf. Imagine, my mother was severely dehydrated, yet there were no liquids or straws at her bedside. Father was a surgeon, not a nurse.

I took out the package of straws, ready to use the rest sparingly because I realized that I would be prioritizing my time for the next few weeks. There would be little opportunity to go shopping. Armed with several straws to keep at her bedside, I leaned over the empty half of the bed with her cup and she drank a few sips with the straw. I waited. She started breathing deeper. I told her how glad I was that she let me look after her and she smiled. She turned a bit. I asked her if she would let me make her comfortable in the pillows and she said, "yes."

This was where my training in Amsterdam kicked in, and I realized quite quickly that I was crucial to my mother's recovery. Let me be clear: In my parents' time of need, I was thrilled that it was me that they had called upon. I was confident that I would be able to nurse my mother back to health. When we were younger, my mother taught us that the mind and the body work together. My mother had "given up" in her mind, and as a result, her body was giving up too. My father knew this and was paralyzed by anxiety. I made it my mission to nurse her back to health.

When my mother finally agreed to drink some fluids, she gave me the message that she had a will to live. Next, she graduated to arrowroot biscuits, which was followed by chicken broth. Eventually she ate rice in the broth, after which she graduated to solid foods like chunks of home cooked chicken soup. I was giving her foods that she normally wouldn't be eating. This was intended to decrease the inflammation of the bowel and give the body much needed nourishment at the same time. Each day, my mother was slowly gaining ground.

On that first evening, she asked me to please stay and sleep beside her. Father never came up to the room that evening and I assumed that he had fallen asleep in his chair. Although reluctant, I acquiesced to lying beside my mother. I had heavy dreams that night. I confess that it was very difficult to sleep next to a dying body. I prayed silently while I was next to her and asked God to please let her recover, if that was His will.

I want to share with you something that's very private about that night: While we were sleeping, my essence was being transferred to my mother. I could feel it. It was a very demanding effort for me while asleep. When I was awake, it was easy to look after my mother. Our bonding was precious and I was very grateful for this opportunity to show her how much I loved her. Even writing about this brings me to tears because it was such a painful thing to do. It was painful because during the time that I slept, my psyche was at its most vulnerable to her influence, and in this gift that I was giving her, I realized that I was in a total loving, forgiving mode. As I was healing her, I was strengthening myself. This was a watershed experience.

As the days went by, sleeping beside my mother night after night, and with her recovery being a certainty, I could relax. There was time for me to place the items that were out everywhere back in the cupboards. My father and I said little to each other; he liked it that way. He saw me work on Moeder and put away the mess, and I could "feel" his approval.

My heavy emotional involvement was lifting with each subsequent day and I relaxed more and more. I was succeeding! Hallelujah! After a few days, Mother was transferred onto a low, comfortable, supportive chair, ensconced in a blanket. This gave me the chance to change and launder the linen. Bed baths had been quick and easy every morning and now her bed would be clean as well. Her strength was improving daily and her sense of humor came back. Her bowels were behaving well, and more and more foods were introduced, one at a time. There were no setbacks and I was very happy and grateful. My prayers were being answered. After about three weeks, I phoned Rob and told him that I was able to come home and we rejoiced. My father and mother were both healthy and happy again and I could go, which I did.

Thankfully, my job was totally supportive of my decisions and I just went right back to work, like I had never been gone. Life was good. Rob and I took a two-week holiday in July of 1969. We drove to Florida and back in Rob's trusty dark blue beetle. Highlights included stops in Savannah, Georgia where we went to the beach, and St. Augustine, Florida where we visited an impressive fort. We also went to the Kennedy Space Center, to Orlando, and to Sanibel Island off the Gulf Coast. All the nature and birds made me vow that we would come back down south to Sanibel Island one day, but we never did.

A few weeks later, in early August, Rob and I were coming back to the cottage from a long canoe trip up the river when I felt a sensation in my abdomen. I knew then that I was pregnant. Once again, my prayers were being answered. I told Rob my news and we marveled at the idea that I could feel my pregnancy just days after our intimacy. We chose a Dutch Gynecologist/Obstetrician and got ready for parenthood. I wanted to work until I was six months pregnant, and I almost made it; however, motherhood would not come easily for me.

I experienced many profound changes during this time in my life. From the elation of my marriage to Rob, to the gratitude of my mother's recovery, and to the blessing of approaching motherhood, I was fully alive. Nursing my mother back to health provided me with a momentous shift in perspective. I was reminded about the importance of family, and was overjoyed to start a family of my very own.

Curtain Calls

- *Enjoy your happiness: It allows you to hope for more happiness in the future, sometimes when you least expect it.*
- *Make family your greatest priority. They are there for you through the good times and the bad.*
- *Giving and receiving with family is meant to foster the greatest feeling of joy. Therefore, enhance, cherish and make the most of the opportunities that arise.*
- *Share your beliefs with those who will listen.*
- *In a marriage, say and do the things that will strengthen the relationship.*

CHAPTER 9

Motherhood and Psychosis
Rears Its Ugly Head

In January of 1970, I was admitted to the third floor of the hospital where I worked. My stomach and back pain were so severe that I needed constant monitoring and care. I was given an ultra sound that looked normal, but obviously something was wrong. On the first day, I was given a strong dose of Donnatal, an anticholinergic/ antispasmic drug that was commonly prescribed at the time. The nursing staff denied my request for pain medicine, much to my dismay. My obstetrician came in each day during the week and I pleaded for relief to no avail. My pain and discomfort were stopping me from being able to sleep and, after twenty minutes of sitting, I would have to get up and walk to relieve the pain. Day after day and night after night, this sequence of events was the same. Each day my fatigue increased. Each night I prayed that the staff would have compassion for me and solve my problem.

Being Bipolar

For seven long days and seven even longer nights, I couldn't sleep. On Monday morning of the eighth day, the obstetrician came in with someone he introduced as Dr. P., a psychiatrist. Dr. P. gently explained that I was bipolar, which meant I had a mental disorder as a result of a chemical imbalance. I was so tired that I could barely lift my chin to look at him. His visit was short and I got a small pill. I went to my private room and was helped into bed; finally, the pain disappeared and I fell asleep. As I was drifting to sleep I remember feeling disgruntled and offended. I had not done this deliberately; I had been begging for help and they had let me suffer!

I said nothing about my new diagnosis because I was too tired to talk. My mother-in-law came to visit and, when she saw that I wasn't eating, she fed me lunch herself. Then she stayed all day so that she could feed me dinner as well. I was so grateful then, and even now her kindness brings tears to my eyes. My mother-in-law came back the next day to feed me breakfast and lunch, and then Rob came to feed me dinner. After that my muscles had recovered. I meditated over what had just happened. At the time, there was no thought that a "bipolar" diagnosis was a life long sentence. I never imagined I would be on medication for 42 years straight before I was mentally strong enough to live without it.

After a few more days of monitoring and stabilizing on the medication, I was discharged. The rest of the pregnancy at home was uneventful, but once May 1970 rolled around, I was fearful. I had gained a little more weight than normal, I sensed that our child was overdue, and once again the doctor wasn't responding to my fears. On May 16th my water broke and the labor pains started. Epidurals for relief were not given because it was thought they might stop the contractions. My labor continued throughout the night, for a total of 27 hours, and I was reliving the nightmare of months earlier.

A Big, Beautiful Baby Boy

I was sweating, exhausted, and barely dilated when the obstetrician decided to do a Caesarian, for which I was extremely grateful. Rob was not allowed in the O.R. and that was a big regret for both of us. We learned later that Peter's head was too large for my pelvis. Since my pelvis was visibly large, the doctor had not expected any difficulties. Peter's head showed the strain of the ill-fitting experience.

When Peter was born, I didn't see him because I was under a general anesthetic. Because it was a caesarian birth, Peter was in the incubator for 24 hours. He filled the space, touching at the top and bottom of the incubator: He was 10 lbs. 8 oz.! Rob and I were so happy and proud, and I was in awe. From one sperm and one egg, this beautiful, healthy baby boy was developed and born. The love that we felt for our "little" baby was all encompassing.

When Rob drove Peter and I home a few days later, I was scared stiff. What if I did something wrong? There was so much to do! Because I was on anti-psychotic medication, breastfeeding was not an option. This was hard because it was an experience that I had so dearly wanted for my child and myself. Peter was crying a lot, day and night. Holding him in my arms didn't soothe him, so we had to go for car rides to calm him down. When we saw the pediatrician, we were told that he had colic due to being intolerant to the usual formulas. We purchased a soy-based powder and made it into a formula with water, and over the weeks his colic eased.

A few weeks after Peter was born, I had an appointment with an M.D. who specialized in endocrinology. He informed me that I would be a diabetic within ten years based on his research and statistics related to other women having birthed a baby of Peter's size. This bad news proved to be inconsequential. The prediction of a doctor or specialist can sometimes be wrong because to this day, I'm the only one of my siblings who doesn't have diabetes!

We found a good caregiver and I was very comfortable leaving Peter with her when I returned to work. I wanted to be self-employed at the Community Nursing Registry of Ottawa, and grateful when I was accepted as a member. This was just my cup of tea! I was looking forward to starting my "normal" life with my husband, my child, and my career.

In February 1971, my parents came to stay with us for a few weeks while they were looking for a house where my father could set up his medical practice. We had quickly purchased a bed for our small third bedroom, and were ready to help. My suicidal thinking, which had been getting worse ever since the third day after Peter's birth, was shoved aside. I refused to give it any further thought when it popped into my head. The problem was that it would pop in more and more often. I shared this issue with no one.

Manic Madness

Father purchased a house in Bourget, a 30-minute drive south east of where we lived. He agreed to my having a weekly weight loss program at a separate clinic space that he had rented. We started working together and I promptly had my second manic episode, for which I needed hospitalization. This was in April 1971, two months after my parents had moved back to Ontario, and 15 months after my first manic episode.

If ever I held any doubts about my diagnosis, this episode sure stopped that thinking. I remember when I was admitted—it was a Friday, and I was desperate to speak with a doctor. I was told that no doctor would see me until I was a patient for about a week. Good behavior would be rewarded. I felt awful that this was the policy in place. It made me feel like a second-class citizen. I already knew that there was a stigma about mental illness. I got a negative or silent reaction from friends and family when I told them why I had been hospitalized. I think it was during this week that I was first placed on lithium. Within days, I noticed the effect on my brain. I felt like I had been lobotomized, chemically.

If I remember correctly, the doctor finally interviewed me on Wednesday. It was then that I declared for the first time that I was Jesus.

I had thought it previously, and had been pleased with myself that I was able to keep the secret. The doctor took a lot of notes, didn't look at me, and when I went into an explanation as to why and how I came to that belief, there was no response. Of course I knew that delusional thinking and grandiose thinking were considered part of the symptoms. I also knew that I considered my thinking to be rational. If this doctor chose to believe what he did, that was a choice that he was allowed to make—I knew who I was. Once I shared that I was Jesus, I declared my divinity each time I was in an episode. These aspects are important because they are the same throughout all of my manic outbursts.

This delusion just came to me one day, and suddenly I understood that I was the physical Jesus who would return as a thief. It was funny because so many people were expecting Jesus to return in His male form, yet I was a female. I asked God how it could possibly be me. I had been damaged before birth when my mother was malnourished during the Dutch hunger winter. God replied that I was deliberately chosen because my mother was malnourished after a second horrific world war. I believe that my damaged brain was the principal reason for my delusional thinking.

Then I asked, "How can I possibly be chosen when my brain doesn't even hold a lot of knowledge?" Again, God answered that there were many knowledgeable people who would believe in me when the time came. I considered it rude for me to keep on questioning God's choices, so I rejoiced in the knowledge, and as the records show, I couldn't keep it to myself every time I went manic. It is very possible that I am one of the falsely declared "daughters" of God. (Many will declare themselves to be Jesus just before His return). Only God knows.

My hospitalization didn't stop me from being excited and happy about my new divine discoveries. It wasn't long before I realized that the professionals no longer held any respect for me—I had lost all credibility. Next came the painful task of persevering in telling myself that I was still worth loving, even though I had just been totally demoralized. After sharing and comparing experiences with other patients on the floor, I discovered that my treatment package was not unusual.

The room where the most comfortable conversations were held was the "smoking" room. I didn't smoke, but whenever I was awake and felt lonely, the smoking room held the vibration of love and comfort that resonated with me. Of course, the terminology that I just used is current terminology. In the early 70's, I couldn't express myself. There was no interest from the staff to have any meaningful communication. The doctor was treating me like a maniac whose symptoms would tell him where the treatment would go next. In the seventies, only other mentally ill patients understood the stigma that was felt by all those who were diagnosed psychotic.

Insomnia was part of my difficulty. Another symptom was an increased appetite. Eating more made me gain weight, but I wasn't in a position to deny myself. My brain felt active, I felt alive, and I loved the feeling. However, not sleeping well was a torture that I never wanted to experience again; I would follow any program that would prevent that from happening. Showering or having a bath several times a day was a pampering that soothed my soul. These people did not know my history and I was not going to explain myself. I wanted to allow my spirituality free reign. Just to myself, I said that all that I was going through was deliberate—the universe wanted me to have these painful experiences so that I would become spiritually stronger.

Trying to Cope

Once I was discharged from The Royal Ottawa Hospital (exclusively for psychiatric patients), my experience was barely discussed. I felt like Rob didn't understand the mental trauma that I had just been forced to endure. He had visited me often, and he was loving and open to my explanations;

nevertheless, I felt a growing frustration with him. I went through the motions of caring for Peter, and sometimes I was overwhelmed with love. I broke into tears when I was alone due to all the mental pain that I was feeling, but I shared that with no one. After all, nest sharing was nothing new for me. There was no memory of the past; there was no hope for the future.

One night, I lost my patience with Rob and threw plates on the kitchen floor. I wasn't content or comforted by his neutral reaction so a few evenings later, I picked up a pointed, serrated 8" kitchen knife and waved it in a circular motion a foot away from Rob in an effort to get the response that I needed from him. He showed more fearless neutrality, which agitated me all the more. The reaction that I needed wasn't happening so I threw the knife on the counter, grabbed the car keys, some clothes and drove away. Rob was left to look after Peter and phone my parents to say I wouldn't be at work the next day.

I went to the Y downtown and swam in the pool for a few hours. After that, I applied for a job as a swimming instructor and I was accepted. In the lounge, I met a blind man and struck up a friendship. He invited me to his apartment and I went. We were intimate that night, and in the morning I put on a different outfit that I had with me. I went to the Y to teach my first swimming lesson and discovered that I had already been fired. Someone had seen my behavior with the regular member and realized that I was in no condition to have any responsibilities. This shock made me realize that I had been irresponsible. I drove home, and asked Rob to forgive me for leaving. I didn't tell him about my unfaithful behavior; it was my secret and I didn't feel good about it. It was more difficult for me to ignore my suicidal thinking, but I kept moving forward and didn't share my thoughts with anyone.

Going to my parents' home every weekday was a welcome relief that gave me a purpose. My parents were both happy to see me every time and we had lots of great conversations about our collective future. Father saw about five patients a day and he had hired a receptionist. She was French Canadian and most of his patients were French Canadian as well. My French was a challenge and she would help me translate sometimes. Father asked me to dispense the medications that he was prescribing. I was uncomfortable with doing this task, but he assured me that this was an acceptable request.

For the following year, we had a routine that brought us many happy memories. Rob and I were totally reconciled. I was so grateful and happy that he had forgiven me, and Peter was an added joy to our lives. Then I discovered that I was pregnant again. The intra uterine- device (IUD) that I was wearing had failed. I meditated on this and talked with Rob about this dilemma. I was convinced that the level of suicidal thinking that I was barely coping with would kill both the fetus and myself were I to continue with the pregnancy. I was so very embarrassed at the idea of going to the local hospital to be assessed for approval of something that would be horribly painful for me to go through with in the first place. I would be a murderer—it was so personal and painful. I am so grateful that Rob understood the reality of my mental pain.

Continuing with the pregnancy was not in question. I went to my father with my dilemma and I felt his love and understanding; it was a welcome relief. The pregnancy was aborted. The relief and the pain of the loss were wrapped up in severe suicidal strain. My assessments of my own mental capacity were correct because a few months later, I attempted suicide by taking a whole bottle of pills. Peter was with the babysitter when Rob came home from work and found me crazed. I was not coherent, and refused to go to the hospital. Rob called the ambulance and by the time it arrived, I had lost consciousness. Rob told me later that my stomach was pumped and the doctors were ambiguous about the ingested contents. My medications were adjusted and I was sent home after three weeks. This was considered my third manic attack.

After my second serious attempt at suicide, I gave staying alive a lot of thought. Of course, I didn't give in to despair deliberately— I loved Rob and Peter beyond reason. It was the pain I was feeling mentally that I found increasingly impossible to bear. This was a pain that existed in my own brain and had nothing to do with external influences. Maintaining my respect for the professionals was easy. I loved my immediate family and my extended family. No one was at fault.

Signs from the Universe

When I went back to work, I could feel that the vibration in my father's office had changed. My father was depressed, but he did not share his struggle. One morning my mother came rushing down the stairs in a panic. She said my father was blue-gray and not breathing. I ran upstairs and found him lying on his back on the bed. His skin color was a definite blue, and his chest was not rising and falling. His mouth was wide open and I could see that his tongue was flaccid and had fallen back. He would need to be turned onto his side. When I tried to turn his torso, I discovered that he was a dead weight, so I had to start with his legs first. Because he was heavy, I had to climb onto the bed in front of him to roll him toward me. His tongue fell forward, and miraculously I watched his normal color return. His pulse was good and his blood pressure was acceptable, yet he was still unconscious so I phoned for an ambulance. He went to the Riverside Hospital, and I promptly went manic.

Truly, this was not a deliberate reaction. I had nothing to say when I was admitted. I was oblivious to the policies of care and I got through the system in no time. Of course, my lithium levels were increased. It was the Fall of 1973 and this was the end of my father's career. When I was discharged, I helped my parents move to an apartment in Ottawa. At that point, I'd had four manic episodes in less than four years. It was important for me to figure out what my triggers were so that the frequency of my outbursts would decrease.

In the spring of 1974 I discovered that I was pregnant again. I was loath to do what I had done before. This fetus had made its way past the I.U.D. even though I had a better quality unit. I am a very spiritual person and felt that the universe wanted me to have this baby. I told myself to "suck it up." For the sake of my baby, (I was obviously being given a second opportunity) I needed to work hard at giving this precious life my very best.

New Life

Rob and I went to a new obstetrician and asked him if it would be safe for me to continue the pregnancy given that I was on lithium. I was examined and the I.U.D. was gone. The fetus had gotten rid of it, which I considered a miracle. The doctor considered the fetus safe if I discontinued the lithium immediately; I was glad to do so. I felt more confident this time. The pregnancy was a breeze. My thinking was overwhelmingly positive. Unbelievably, I was excited, happy, and I felt stable.

That year, Rob and I looked at many homes because we hoped moving to the west end would decrease my severe allergies and improve my mental health. We found a house that backed onto parkland with a closing date of Dec. 31, 1974. We weren't worried about how the move would impact the baby. At about 7 months, it was recommended that I go back on lithium, and I did what I was told. I knew of no reason to disobey. As the months went by, I didn't feel the baby kick, but the ultra sounds were normal so there was no need for me to question the easy pregnancy.

My obstetrician was really good and I had faith in his skills. I went into a mild labor on Dec. 15th, but the doctor didn't trust it and scheduled a caesarian for the next day. Paul was born by epidural anesthetic and I was awake to see him enter the world.

He was grey tinged and had a poor Apgar score. An Apgar score is given for five vibrancy signals of the baby multiplied by two. The highest possible score is ten. A score under five is bad news. Paul was under five. My heart went out to him. Our second son had serious health issues and I immediately felt responsible. Had he been through a regular birth experience, he would not have survived it. Shortly after birth, we were told that his prognosis was guarded, which meant that it was possible he could die. But he was a fighter; I could sense that right away.

A number of blood and urine tests were done and the results gave a diagnosis that only a very good pediatrician would detect. He was a doctor from Chile and was in Canada on a sabbatical. We trusted his diagnosis and realized that he was a very good pediaterian. Paul had post-urethral valves which allowed voiding once he was born.. Paul had not voided as a fetus, which destroyed his left kidney, and severely scarred the right. He was given an immediate supra pubic catheter. When he was eight months old, we went to Toronto for surgery done by a very talented urologist who removed the post urethral valves. Unfortunately, this surgery was destined to make Paul incontinent, and it wasn't until he was 18 years old that this issue was resolved by a gadget that had been invented in the States.

During the first year of Paul's life I prayed and prayed and prayed! What amazed me was that I spiritually felt the loss of many parents' little children. I am sharing this for the first time because I consider myself sane. You may consider me eccentric at some point; that is your privilege. Over the years, my faith became even more aggressive, my prayers more fervent. Just as you are allowed to be an atheist or an agnostic, I am allowed to have my own beliefs.

Surviving

I learned over the years that lithium is considered a teratogenic, meaning it alters fetal development. From the first discovery of Paul's health issues, I felt responsible. No matter how many professional people told me that it was not my "fault," I felt responsible for the condition that Paul was in at his birth. During Paul's first few months alive, I decided that from then on, all medical decisions would be either accepted or denied by me. I was responsible for what happened to my body. This meant that I would follow all medical advice, but if I questioned anything, I would investigate it at length, including getting a second opinion.

After Paul's surgery we realized that my pregnancy was easy because Paul had not voided as a fetus. Not moving around in the womb is exactly what had saved his life. Had Paul moved, both his kidneys would have been destroyed beyond survival. The scarred kidney that functioned did so at less than 50% of full capacity. I lived in fear that he was going to need dialysis for the rest of his life. He was conveniently allowed to stay in the hospital while we moved from Blackburn Hamlet to the west end on Dec. 31st.,1974. We loved our new house and Paul was gaining a good color.

Paul was in and out of the hospital for his first few years. The nurses would always tell us what a charmer he was, just like a little doll. After two years, Rob and I were still not sure that Paul's prognosis would improve. We decided that we would try for a third child even with my mental history because if for some reason I improved and Paul didn't, we'd have two children or three, but never just one. Whatever happened, we wanted more than one child. Having children and raising them to the best of our ability was the most wonderful purpose we could ever have.

The last pregnancy gave us our 3rd and last child because my tubes were tied. The pregnancy was similar to the first, which was good news. On May 23rd 1977, I went into labor and was 5 cm. dilated in several easy hours. I was booked for a caesarian delivery just a few days later, but I was immediately hospitalized when the labor started. I was not allowed to deliver the baby naturally because it was considered too dangerous with a risk of uterine rupture. The policy was to give me a liquid by mouth before the caesarian and I refused. The nurse insisted 2 more times and I refused each time. The 4th time I finally said yes because I didn't have the heart to fight any longer.

It was an epidural birth and as I lay open and supine, I retched but I had nowhere to go. I asked for more medication via the epidural and it was given. I retched and retched and thought, why did this policy exist? Why had the staff not recognized that this would be the result? After this incident, no explanation or apology was ever given. I did not fight it. We had a daughter and we were more than thrilled. She was the same birth weight as Paul, 8 lb. 8 oz., and was a healthy happy baby. The amazing thing was that ten days after we were all at home, I started lactating and began to breastfeed. Little Mary enjoyed her feedings and so did I. Miracles do happen.

I love that I am able to write this book. After being hospitalized ten times for going manic, and being an in-patient each time for three or four weeks, I'm thrilled to be able to share with you what I have put behind me. You too can put any adversity behind you. If I can do it with my history, you can do it too. Find what you love, identify your purpose, and spread joy. Focus on the positive and have faith that you will overcome the negative.

Curtain Calls:

- *Give your beliefs some thought, so that you understand why you believe what you do.*
- *Tolerate the beliefs of others.*

— *Foster love. If having children is not of interest to you, find family or friends who complete your life. Socialize and give joy, abundance, and purpose.*

— *Accept the physical and mental health issues of those you love and show empathy for what they experience.*

CHAPTER 10

Environmental Sensitivities

Having two out of five family members with significant health issues, mine mental and Paul's physical, was a daily struggle within our family unit. However, Rob and I were undeterred in our determination to have a close, happy family. After all, we both had lots of love to give our children. Unfortunately, everyone was on my roller coaster, and the instability was real. Rob acted as our stable force. Paul's health issues were affecting his brother and sister; he used them to take out his frustration with his physical struggles, and at the time did not share his feelings. This is what happens in so many families when there is a child with challenges: the dynamics with siblings is more intense. All three of our children like their privacy and although they have supported me with writing this book, Rob and I know that they prefer to keep their personal matters to themselves. It's not that they're ashamed of me; it's just that there are some memories that they would rather not go back to—this means that the good memories are left untouched as well.

Healthcare

Dr. S., who did such a great surgery on Paul when he was eight months old, moved to Ottawa shortly after the Toronto surgery so that Paul had continuous excellent care. Paul also had an excellent nephrologist, Dr. W., who lived in the area. These two doctors looked after him for his first 18 years, and for this we are ever grateful. When Paul was three, Dr. S. successfully did a left nephrectomy (removal of the destroyed left kidney). He was too young to tolerate the surgery before this age. When Paul was 12, 13, and 14 years old, I was especially nervous because this was when he could start needing dialysis. When Paul and I went to his doctor visits, and when he was sometimes tested or hospitalized on the urology unit, we saw young teenagers on dialysis and it broke my heart. I prayed that Paul would have smooth sailing, and he did. I thanked God for what I saw as a miracle. There were so many visits to CHEO (Children's Hospital of Eastern Ontario) over those years. The entire surrounding community of Ottawa/Gatineau strongly supports our children's hospital and I am extremely thankful for each and every contribution or show of support.

After Paul's Toronto surgery, I developed a benign goiter. The lithium in my system caused the goiter, and thus the lithium was discontinued. That was in late 1975. Boy, was I happy! No more taking that hated drug. I have been on a number of effective antipsychotics since, and all were a whole lot better for my mind than lithium. The goiter destroyed my thyroid and I've been on synthetic thyroxin ever since. There was never a time that I did not take my antipsychotics. I knew that they were my best defense for not having another manic episode.

Holland

In June of 1975, the four of us went to visit Tante Jannie and Oom Cees. It was a wonderful "fix" for me. By "fix" I mean that seeing Tante Jannie and Oom Cees at the Aardhuis was like getting a big dose of fresh air after being oxygen deprived for ten years. T.J. and O.C. gave us a unique gift during our three weeks with them: They offered to look after the children while we went on a three-day holiday to Paris, France. We were happy to accept, and had a glorious, memorable little "honeymoon." When we returned refreshed and relaxed, Tante Jannie told us the story of Prince Bernard's visit. Peter had made a set up using little sticks on the driveway and as the prince walked by, Peter said, "Don't step on my runway!" Prince Bernard replied with a chuckle in perfect English, "I'll be careful." And Peter never realized that he got an answer in his own language, in a foreign country, from a real prince! Unfortunately, Peter barely remembers this private audience.

Complications

After the birth of each child, there were more and more difficulties with my lower back. I would feel a prolonged severe pain on many days, aggravated by lifting the children. I was relieved when my general practitioner finally diagnosed me, in 1976, as having a severe degenerated disc between L4 and L5. I finally had a legitimate reason for my back pain, and thus felt validated, which gave me permission to look after my back however needed. At the time there was no solution for relief of my back pain, so looking for the solution rather than putting on a short-term Band-Aid was a focus for me in those years.

My father went with me in the late '70's to a surgeon at the Ottawa Civic Hospital, my favorite local tertiary hospital. The Dr. told me that my pain and sciatica would resolve itself once I had lost a few pounds. (I was overweight at this point and 20 years later, I was obese, having lost the battle with weight loss). The Dr. repeated that I was not a candidate for back surgery because it would only develop scar tissue that would continue to cause pain. I was deeply disappointed because living with chronic severe pain made it more difficult to share happiness with the children. I loved them, which meant that every morning I woke up resolved to give them my best, no matter what. Pain management clinics did not yet exist. When asked, all three of my children said that they remember no periods of prolonged pain or depression, just the chaos of when I went manic.

Back pain wasn't my only health problem; I also had terrible allergies. I had conventional allergy testing done, but the results were negative. I didn't accept the outcome because I *knew* that I had lots of allergies. I kept asking and looking and eventually found Dr. G. — she discovered allergies and prescribed treatments, but I still felt that something was missing. My faithful hairdresser told me about Dr. Molot, an environmental ecologist and M.D. who focused on the effects of the environment on a person's health. His testing showed that I had mood alterations due to sublingual triggers. Finally, we were on to something! He took a long time to gather the medical history of each of our children and myself. The questions that he asked were hitting home. Over time we were given a series of injections, and we also religiously followed a significant diet change. I noticed a distinct mood improvement in all of us. It was such a relief that health wise, we were getting somewhere. I am forever grateful to Dr. Molot for solving the mystery of my allergies.

Color Codes

Living in the west end of Ottawa did reduce the frequency of my manic episodes to once every 3 years or so, and after Dr. Molot started his treatments, the frequency was reduced even more to every 8 years or so. Rob and I had set up a system. He would tell me whether he saw me as being green, amber, or red. Green meant that I was quite safe, mentally. Amber meant that he could see some "warning" signs; signs for me to be alert and improve my coping mechanisms. Red meant that I needed to be hospitalized because I had gone manic again. The system worked well and it gave us a better sense of control within the family. As the years went by, Rob and I became more experienced at adjusting my moods, which was done by using better communication tools.

There were many times that I went to amber for various lengths of time before I went back to green again. When Rob and I had an argument about something, I was always overly passionate about my point of view. One of the main markers for my mania was that intense passion. Often, my passion would awaken Rob's fear of another manic episode, given that he had seen me go manic so quickly on several occasions. Despite the many times that I was in amber, Rob did not stop me from doing some volunteering so that I remained somewhat active and productive. While Mary was in nursery school for two years, I volunteered to be the school's registrar. When Mary turned six, I became Brown Owl for the local Brownie unit for five years. I worked very hard at staying stable.

Career Woman

After Paul and Mary were born, I did not work for 10 years. As a result, I was not confident when I went back to work. Over the years, Dr. Molot helped me feel strong enough to be productive in the labor force again. I went back to work as a graduate nurse with a company called ParaMed, and that gave me a smooth transition from housewife to career woman. At the company Christmas party in 1991, I met someone who encouraged me to re-apply for membership with the C.N.R.O. I sent a letter to the Ontario Nursing Registry and asked what steps I needed to take to work as an R.N. again. The reply was that I could go ahead and start working as a R.N. right away! I was overjoyed. After being with ParaMed for seven years, from 1984 to 1991, I started working as a self employed R.N. at the Community Nursing Registry of Ottawa. In Feb. 1994, after 354 hours of courses in Multidiscipline Palliative Care, I received a certificate with Honors from Algonquin College. I specialized in palliative care nursing for the last seven years of my career until I retired in 2001. I was thrilled with this responsibility and freedom.

Caregiving

Throughout these years, I experienced an underlying and continuous low-grade suicidal thinking. That struggle of thought would be more prevalent when I was in amber. My first response at amber was to decrease my "stimulation," i.e. no listening to music or the radio and less communication with others. Rob noticed that regularly I would need to present my own way of thinking, since I was a very poor listener. Sometimes I gave myself an afternoon nap. When I was in amber, Rob said it took him back to the days when he saw me visibly closer to acting on my suicidal thinking. It made him feel very nervous and anxious, and he immediately wanted to calm things down. At first he would feel disturbed, and then if I didn't respond to his efforts, it would escalate to feelings of desperation and anxiety.

As you're reading this, the reality of Rob being my caregiver more than, or as much as, my husband becomes apparent. Years ago, I realized that I wanted to let Rob know how much I appreciated what he was doing for me, year after year. I resolved to let him know as much as possible, so he hears "I love you, Rob", every night before we go to sleep. In the beginning, there were many nights when he said nothing back, and I resolved to say nothing about his silence because his actions spoke louder than his words. Over time, I expressed my desire to hear him say something nice in return. He complied and said, "I love you." I could feel that it was sometimes a routinely given reply, but that "crumb" was all I needed.

As mentioned earlier, Rob and the children remember seeing no periods of visible depression in me, only times of being in amber and going towards red. Going to red and needing hospitalization usually happened within a 2-day period. This meant that the entire family would be on eggshells every time I was in amber. During these periods the anxiety ran high. The most difficult memories for Rob were the earliest frequent manic episodes where I refused to go to the hospital and refused to let Rob be my caregiver. It deeply hurt his feelings when I angrily rejected him as my husband in those early years. I am aware of Rob's level of commitment to our marriage, and his level of forgiveness; words cannot express my gratitude for his unwavering support.

Advice

There is something important that I want to share here. When looking at stories on the news, I see family members in anguish over their loved one who committed suicide and left no note. I would not have left a note had I ever succeeded in committing suicide. Don't blame yourself if there is no suicide note, and don't blame yourself if the person who died incriminates you. I venture to say that almost the entire struggle your loved one had was due to his/her own thinking. When a mind is chemically imbalanced, it is hard for that person to get through what is so destructive, so mentally painful. Their fight was internal, not with you. When I was suicidal, I only wanted to escape "ME." I realized that my own thinking was poisonous to my being, and I grieved at the reality of not being able to get away from "myself." Please, if anyone you know or loved has ever committed suicide, remember that their struggle was their own.

The Joys of Children

Rob, Peter, Paul and I went on holiday to Disneyworld in Florida in December of 1978. Peter and Paul snuck out of our room on the first morning that we were there, and we didn't know it until two policemen knocked on our door. Peter was seven and Paul would celebrate his fourth birthday while we were there. Peter had taken Paul to the small river next to our hotel. Luckily, the officers saw them and quickly brought them back. They said, "Did you know that the river had alligators in it?" It never crossed our mind that the boys would leave our room in the morning before we woke up, let alone almost get eaten by alligators!

All of Rob's and my children have their own unique personalities, yet they also share a common thread. Peter has a gentle kind soul that gives him a very mild nature. He has great management skills that were developed and fine-tuned in his role as the eldest child. Paul is a force to be reckoned with; he still fights each day of his life to get the most out of every hour. He has a wicked sense of humor and he's a great manager as well. Mary is another gentle soul just like Peter, and she has the gift of patience. She is a great manager as well. Isn't it interesting that all three are great managers? There is no such thing as coincidence. Although we all have a freedom of choice, the Universe is unfolding just as it should, and I am so content that all three of my children are solid, productive, happy adults. Rob and I are so proud of them.

Blessings

In my Palliative Care nursing career, I noticed that the patients who had a strong spiritual belief system were the ones who had the most amazing and peaceful journeys toward their last breath. My numerous encounters with death and my defiance of the lure of death made me feel very comfortable with this field of nursing. My comfort level allowed me to offer my services and be grateful when the feedback was a return of what I had given. Palliative Care was a wonderfully rewarding career.

Family Dynamics

On July 31st, 1981, my entire immediate family celebrated my parent's 50th wedding anniversary at a weekend retreat along the northern shores of Lake Ontario. These family members included three generations of parents, children, and grandchildren. Upon our arrival, Rob was promptly stung by a bee and was bedridden for almost the entire weekend. All three of the children did enjoy the occasion, but I missed Rob. A few days later, I was back at the Royal Ottawa Hospital for a month. What I concluded from that experience was that I needed to be careful when participating in family functions. The many social interactions must have triggered a very old weakness that I didn't tolerate. A word of advice—if you have stressors that cause physical or mental setbacks, don't deny the need to be good to yourself. You must learn to give yourself permission to retreat when necessary.

I didn't tell my family that I suspected my hospital admission was directly related to social stressors at the retreat. I didn't want them to think that they were responsible for my manic attack. I considered this social weakness to be something that I needed to mentally accept so that I could stay away from the stressors. Giving yourself the space to be who you are without having to explain it to anyone is an extremely useful tool. My almost daily suicidal thinking was something that I had learned to live with, and it didn't frighten me anymore. I felt the constant comfort of God at my side.

Non-Judgment

I realized in the mid 80s that anything to do with religion was a trigger, given my delusions. However, I am now comfortable sharing that I constantly feel God and Jesus at my side. A few months ago I read the book, *Conversations With God*, written by Neale Donald Walsch. He has written seven more books along the same line. He is mentally sane and his books are well received. Thus, being considered delusional and manic is not directly related to my religious beliefs. I need not consider myself a religious fanatic. Anyone who calls me a religious fanatic is passing judgment, and we are not meant to judge each other. Personally, I would love to be in a non-judgmental society where everyone loves, and lets their inner light shine for all to enjoy.

When I gave Dr. Molot my physical and mental history, I did not share any information about my religious beliefs. I didn't share it during my monthly visits to the psychiatrist, either. As far as my psychiatrist knew, I had forgotten the details of my delusions. Even though I didn't speak of it, religion was still a central theme in my life and manic episodes. If this information is of any benefit to you, then my sharing this very personal subject has been of value. Please learn from my experience and do not fear judgment. It is best to just be honest with yourself and those who are trying to help you.

In the 80s, I was actively looking for what would improve my life, and in turn improve the lives of all those who were in my sphere. My focus was on my husband and children's happiness and well-being. Re-igniting my nursing career turned out to be a huge benefit for the whole family. Even though I still struggled with suicidal thoughts, my manic episodes had decreased and I was remaining stable for longer and longer periods of time. I am so grateful to everyone who helped support me along the way.

Curtain Calls:

- *Old habits die-hard; however, you CAN train your mind to adopt new and healthy practices. Even if your improved direction of thought is done in baby steps, know that you're moving beyond habits that no longer serve you.*

— *Your husband (or wife) deserves your greatest emotional effort. A good marriage doesn't just "happen." First, be aware of how much you love yourself. If you discover that you need to forgive yourself for something, know that the universe is listening and that you are forgiven, if you will allow it. Thus, loving yourself becomes easier. If you don't have love of self, you can't give love. Generosity allows you to give your love to others.*

— *After your spouse, give your best to your children every day. They are your top priority and the attention that you generously give them will come back ten-fold over time.*

— *After your spouse and children, give time to your parents and the rest of your family. Time is your most precious commodity. You must spend time with them and take care of them as they progress into old age. Taking care of your parents will bring a great deal of rewards that will become apparent once the "work" of it is over.*

— *If you are under the care of a professional, a psychologist or a psychiatrist, you will get help only when you are willing to share. First, there needs to be a solid connection and bond of trust. Then, if the answers you're getting don't square up for you, be polite with saying that you would like to keep on looking for someone until you find the person who "fits" you. You have a right to choose the professional who is going to help you with painful memories/thoughts. Don't be timid about this — your mental health directly impacts your quality of life.*

CHAPTER 11

Palliative Care Nursing and Reiki

When my second manic episode happened in the spring of 1971, Rob and I decided that we were not going to let it stop us from enjoying our lives together. This episode had worn me down and shown me that my psychosis was a real illness that demanded attention. Regardless, we had a trip to Holland and England planned, and nothing was going to stop us from seeing our relatives. My spring hospitalization was downplayed because my mental illness need not be discussed. In 1971, I barely remember seeing T.J. and O.C. It was the hospitalization and the short visit with them that gave me few memories. Forgetting that summer trip to Holland and England shows you how memories can get buried. Thankfully, as mentioned earlier, in 1975 I got the "satisfying fix" of being in Holland with T.J. and O.C. when Rob and I, and our two boys, had a focused trip that provided a comforting familial emotional connection: it's still a beautiful memory today.

Love Beyond Reason

Tante Jannie told me again and again over the years that I was not allowed to cry when I phoned her or when I finally saw her in person. Each time, it was a very difficult request for me to fulfill. The depth of sadness that

I felt when I heard her voice on the phone was intolerable for me, but I wasn't allowed to express that feeling. After the call I would make sure I was alone so that no one would see or hear me, and I would cry bitter tears. I loved and missed T.J. beyond reason. In hindsight, I know now that she had a brain tumor from the late eighties into the nineties, and a huge amount of steroids and other powerful drugs were administered that put her into a remission from the cancer. How much did our love for each other contribute to her miracle recovery? She never shared this with me, but I knew that she had gained a lot of weight, and it was to the point that I was afraid to visit. Her physical image had changed so much, and I didn't think I could accept this new image in my mind. My fear was that it would alter my love for her, and it was overwhelming. Sometimes I wondered whether our relationship was more important to me than to her. But I respected her a great deal and I had many questions that I left unasked because I waited for her to tell me what she was willing to share.

Tante Jannie's unique personality was magnified by the love that many people of all ages had for her. She was a spiritual mother to me and at least four other people, all of whom were drawn to Tante Jannie just like I was. I loved that she shared this talent with others. She was a wonderful, gifted role model and yet she remained very humble in her being. Among other things, she shared with me how she felt about Oom Cees, and I felt privileged to hear her most private thoughts. She would tell me that someday she would talk to me from a cloud, and with her arms she would draw a picture of a little cloud above her head.

Royal Holiday

In 1979 Rob went to a conference in Poland, while Peter, Paul, Mary and I went straight to Tante Jannie and Oom Cees in Holland. We all had a holiday at the beach on the North Atlantic Ocean near the popular Dutch resort town of Schreveningen. Rob joined us for the last day. The

Gulf Stream allows the water to feel warm even though Holland lies pretty far north. I was in heaven and will forever fondly remember this moment in time. The large multi-family sized building that we stayed at was exclusively for employees of the Dutch royal family. It has since burned down, so sadly this haven cannot be revisited.

Grandeur and Delusion

Right after my parents had their 50th wedding anniversary in July of 1981, I was hospitalized for going manic and was back on the fifth floor of the Royal Ottawa Hospital. Trying to hold myself together during the anniversary gave me social triggers that I tried to ignore. Instead of being able to absorb the stress, I ended up manic, declaring myself as Jesus Christ after hospital admission. I could go from being "normal" to being manic in as little as two-days. This happened in part because I got emotional and was unable to control my behavior. For me, there is nothing pleasant about being in a state of mania. My thoughts move faster, my speech becomes short and choppy, I need fewer hours of sleep, and I have thoughts of grandeur and delusion. In a mania attack, I am aggressive, as it is part of my symptomatology. However, as the years go by, I am less and less interested in confrontational exchanges. Also, I am now able to recognize for myself when I'm moving into "amber" so that I "put the brakes" on myself.

Conversations with God

By the early 80s, I was discouraged with being in a mental institution time and again. There was always the horrible long wait before seeing a psychiatrist. I wanted professional emotional support and wasn't getting it. I wonder if better therapeutic psychological support is available to patients today. I remember vividly how I felt, being left at loose ends. I knew that my spirituality was not to be indulged. For almost ten years, from 1982 on, I did not allow myself any "Conversations with God." However, while I was in the hospital, my spirituality had free reign. It was safe for me to share my love for Jesus while I was sick. While I was delusional I wasn't afraid of making mistakes, and I felt right at home in the hospital. Outside the hospital setting, I felt like an oddball. I had a fear of social rejection because I knew that I was different from people I met. When Rob was editing this chapter, he questioned this fear. In his view, he didn't see me ever show any fear of socializing, and said he saw me from day one as being fairly normal. I am very pleased to hear it!

Shikun Oz

In 1982 my parents moved into a new apartment building called "Shikun Oz." This was an apartment building built to house mostly Jewish seniors. "Shikun Oz" means "House of God" for those of the Jewish faith. Over the years there have been many relatives and friends who lived in this building. I was thrilled that my parents had moved because "Shikun Oz" was conveniently close to me. I wanted to continue to be their main caregiver. My sister, who also lived in Ottawa, visited my parents faithfully as well, so my parents had their two youngest children visiting them regularly. During these years my father wrote a book (that is also in a PDF format) called "A History of the Family Trip over 500 years." He diligently researched a vast amount of information (this was before the age of search engines) and collated it for posterity. My mother in turn, enjoyed going to the local grocery store that was only a few hundred meters from her door. She used a buggy that would roll her purchases behind her. Both of my parents were happy with the move, and our relationship strengthened due to their closer proximity.

Escape

From 1982 to 1991 I was finally free of frequent manic episodes thanks to following the measures provided by Dr. Molot. My bouts of crying and feeling depressed were done in the privacy of my bedroom when I was alone. Finally being able to hide my emotional pain gave me a sense of control. When all three of my children recently told me that they had not noticed my periods of depression, I was really pleased. It shows my efforts were successful and that means a lot to me. Feeling suicidal was still a part of the depression. My escape was in reading Harlequin romances. There was a bookstore next to the grocery store (selling new and used books) and I bought romances weekly. When I was back in the work force, my own money was paying for my "love addiction" and I felt good about that. The 187 pages followed a familiar formula that gave a consistency to my emotional life.

Taking a Stand

In the 70s, Rob and I not only had marriage counseling for two years, but we also diligently both implemented the "rules." Both of us were rewarded with a marriage that developed a strong foundation. Our marriage has been solid ever since. It all has to do with good communication, respecting each other, appreciating each other, and nurturing our love for each other. One of the things that Rob and I have in common is our taste in T.V. programs. We both like watching current news. I often see mentally ill people who are on trial for being violent with their immediate families. Thankfully, being violent has never been part of who I am. Even when I went manic, there was never any question of violence. Thus, I disagree when I see the courts give lighter sentences to those that are deemed "not criminally responsible" individuals. I look forward to the day when such criminals will have the correct mental health support while being incarcerated for a time *equal* to someone who is considered mentally sane. The prison time may be served in gentler surroundings to compensate for their mental disorders.

Church Goer

After my parents moved nearby in 1982, I went to the Ottawa Mennonite Church with my father for three years. We went to this church because my father was a Mennonite, but eventually I left the community because it was not completely in line with my thinking. Sometimes Rob and the children came, but never my mother. It was my first time in church since I was a passionate, emotionally unstable teen. This time with father, I remember holding back the tears when I tried to sing a hymn. It would take another book to explain what went through my mind on those mornings. Thankfully, no one noticed my emotional passion. Finally, I am at a point today where my heightened emotion that erupted so easily over the years is under control. No one is more pleased than I am.

Palliative Care

In 1985 I started working for ParaMed as a graduate nurse. I spent seven years with this company and then became a self- employed Registered Nurse. A lot of my patients over these years were palliative and I wanted to learn more about this aspect of nursing so that I could give better service. My parents and Godparents also stood to benefit from the new knowledge. It took from September 1991 to February 1994 to complete the 354 hours required for the Multidiscipline Palliative Care Course at Algonquin College. This was a program that had only been in place for a few years. One of my teachers was a very dynamic woman who taught me that it was safe to be myself. She was the first person I met who openly taught us to love ourselves. The permission to express my feelings felt like a dam breaking open.

Reiki

In my Palliative Care program, we were told about a healing modality that was spiritual in nature, but was also non-denominational. It involved an energy awareness that could be fostered and given to recipients with a hands-off approach. This universal energy was called Reiki. I was fascinated. The Reiki Master teacher, Jacqueline Fairbrass, lived in Blackburn Hamlet where we used to live. I registered and joined a class of ten men and women for a daylong course in the first level of Reiki. Practitioners invoke the energy from within; we all have an energy that we can share. With my patients, I didn't have to ask because their spirit would tell me whether they would like to receive this gift of energy.

Self-Help

All of the various classes in Reiki and Palliative Care opened a new world for me. I realized that since the mid 80s, with the help of Dr. Molot, I had been trying to improve my mental health on my own. And I was succeeding. The courses only helped me to improve. We started by reading self help books. First, we all read the books written by the trailblazer, Elizabeth Kubler-Ross; next we read Bernie S. Siegel books; and we also read *You can Heal Your Life*, by Louise L. Hay. In class we reviewed how we interpreted the writings. Being able to read those books thrilled me because for years attempts to read those genres of books were aborted because they were too heavy for me. But these palliative care books were unraveling the complexity of my own thinking because they encouraged a discovery of self. I resonated personally with what I was meant to understand with patients.

It became possible for me to think more about others than myself. Spirituality was discussed in a safe environment. One of my teachers, Judy, noticed that I was a very passionate student and she allowed me to make no apologies for it. I was allowed to be emotional. We were allowed to be who we were innately. It was such a welcome relief. This didn't stop me from having excruciatingly painful mental anguish when I was safely alone, but there was finally a light at the end of the tunnel. I realized that the day might come when I was mentally over my brain chemical imbalance. I shared this hope with no one. Who would understand what I was revealing? It was unheard of that anyone who is psychotic ends up recovering after decades of being on medication. When you read my main points consecutively in this book, I believe that you will understand my hope.

Crash

In the summer of 1991, my parents were celebrating their 60th wedding anniversary in British Columbia and they wanted all six of their children to be at this important event. I said that I couldn't come. I knew that I wouldn't be able to tolerate the amount of emotion that would be present. My mother particularly objected to my saying "no." However, neither parent had ever visited me when I was in the hospital, so I felt no discomfort with not explaining myself. They wouldn't understand, but the pressure was there. Then, my brother Pieter spoke up and said that in support of me, he would stay home as well. Thus, my parents had only four of their six children at their golden wedding anniversary. Despite my efforts at protecting myself, I crashed. I was in my bedroom as I saw "events" unfold on television that I related to in a distortion of my mind. In a surreal sequence of events, Mary saw me collapse on our bed and then in somewhat of a trance, I went down the stairs to the living room, laid myself on the floor, and outstretched my arms as if I was hanging on the cross. I saw the horrified looks on Mary's, Paul's and Rob's faces. I don't remember if our son Peter was there. The ambulance was called, and I was back at the R.O.H.

Of course I declared myself to be Jesus again, and this time I was given a thorough physical examination shortly after admission. It included looking at my private parts, despite my objections. The indignity of the female doctor who thought a lot of herself was something that I refused to let affect me. I was well aware of the judgment that people felt with psychiatric patients. Silently, I resolved to foster my own skills of non-judgment. I forgave myself for being sick again. This was a shorter stay in hospital, only three weeks; it was just a little blip. I knew the drill; I knew the steps to a faster recovery and I said to myself, "See, imagine how bad my breakdown would have been had I gone to B.C.?" I was very grateful that I was getting to know myself better.

Lessons

There is something important that I will share now. The lessons I had about the dangers of guns, taught by Oom Cees, always stayed front and center with me. When Peter and Paul were little, there was of course a time when they asked for toy guns. I had heard enough stories from my father and O.C. about the Second World War that I wanted my children to have nothing to do with guns. Peter and Paul were not allowed to have any guns, including water pistols. I explained to them why this was such a hard and fast rule, and they walked away from my explanation with frowns on their faces. A few years later, I found a gun made of crudely put together wood pieces and nails. Peter had made that gun and had told me nothing about it! I decided to just let it go. You can imagine what I think of the powerful American Gun Lobby. I believe violence begets violence, and peace begets peace.

Prayer

While I was back in school, Paul was at risk of having a decline of kidney function related to early teen "growth spurts." I prayed for his health and realized how safe it was to pray as often as I liked, and thus I prayed every day. This was another greater freedom that I silently gave myself without any fanfare. To finally have freedom of thought over my spirituality made me say hallelujah! I was not going to worry about the psychiatric consequences of my freedom of choice in thinking. I loved being back in class. I was taught that learning is a good thing to do to keep the mind exercised and healthy. I went to Jacqueline Fairbrass again and with great happiness, took the Reiki level II class.

Methods of Recovery

Jacquie and I had become friends and while I was driving, and showing her what I liked about living in Ottawa, my switch was tripped. It was as easy as that: I had gone manic again. Where did that come from? Was I not allowed to be happy and content? Nonsense. My method of recovery after another short hospital stay worked well. I didn't even record this episode earlier in this book. My control was improving and that meant that I felt better about my bipolar disorder. I was no longer a victim of the disease because I knew that with perseverance, I would conquer it. Decreasing activity and lessening sound stimulation were the main methods that I used to "rest" my mind.

Gift of Love

My palliative care patients were people to whom I could safely give all my feelings of love. These feelings could be accepted or rejected, and it was all done in silence. Especially when one is on their final journey, they deserve to constantly feel that they have freedom over the choices that they are still able to make. I was drawn to this field of nursing because I had stared death in the face so many times. Suicidal thinking had been a mainstay in my life. I had a need to share my gift of love. I realized that it was easy for me to "feel" what others were experiencing emotionally, and that allowed me to speak less. Palliative care patients appreciate it when less is said.

Personal growth can be had by anyone, and if you have reached this far in my book, consider yourself to have grown personally. You have read many pages of a story that may have been hard for you to continue with, in one way or another. My hope is that you will adopt the practice of non-judgment and use this book as a comfort that you are not alone, or as a way to get an objective view of someone who has successfully overcome a severe mental illness.

Curtain Calls

- *If you're living with a chronic illness and you want to find relief, keep looking. With all the tools available on the Internet, you'll likely succeed in finding the information you need to develop a plan.*
- *The universal feeling of love, when fostered within yourself, has the potential to heal. Give the healing gift of love.*
- *Curiosity leads to a desire for knowledge. Brain exercise is as important as physical exercise.*
- *Be responsible for your own body, mind, and spirit. We're constantly told to "check with our doctor." By all means, check with your doctor, but remember that the buck stops with YOU where your body is concerned.*
- *Be non-judgmental. We are all equal in the eyes of our creator. We all have the capacity to love and be loved.*

CHAPTER 12

The 5 P's of Overcoming Depression

In the Fall of 1991, I started the Palliative Care program at Algonquin College. My experience in nursing, and my aging parents, led me to start an in-depth study of the subject. Little did I know that my personal growth would benefit immensely as well! It was during this program that I learned the importance of self-love. In addition to studying Palliative Care, I began a journey into the healing power of Reiki. Meditation was encouraged with Reiki courses, and as a result I started meditating several times a week. The meditating helped me love myself on an even deeper level.

A Difficult Summer

During the summer of 1992, my father had a major heart attack while in a British Columbia hospital emergency room. He was revived and fully recovered. Because neither of my parents ever came to the phone, my oldest brother updated me on the attack and his recovery. In mid-September, my parents drove by car to Calgary and then flew back to Ottawa. They had taken the summer events in stride, and were glad to be back in their apartment enjoying their independence. My mother, sensing the changing times, voiced her desire to never be put in a nursing home.

I tried to help my parents as much as possible with shopping, banking, and general accounting. My brother Pieter had been named the Executor for both parents, and took care to ensure their wills were complete. It was decided that all six children would receive their inheritance while my parents were still alive. My father called this "giving with the warm hand." It was helpful for them because it meant all their affairs were already in order.

My oldest brother, Gus, came to Ontario for New Years a few months later. Our brother Pieter and his wife, Pixie, hosted all six of us siblings while we were celebrating. Our parents were the guests of honor. Because of Father's previous heart attack, Gus wanted to tell our parents in person that they were no longer allowed to come to the "farm" in B.C. Gus hated to give them this news, but the amount of care that our parents needed was more than he and his wife could handle. Both our parents were very disappointed, but realized that their children were right. It was during this trip that, we also came to the agreement that I would be the spokesperson for the family should either our father or mother become a patient in the hospital. I accepted this role, and I was pleased to be asked.

A Declaration of Love

After we celebrated the New Year, and our parents were back in Ottawa, we all talked about how we could help our parents in the best way possible. This was the year that they would both turn 87 years old. My brother and sisters and I all got along well until the last evening. Enjoying the ambience and the company was heady for me. All six of us were emotional and passionate. I felt such a love for all present and when we were alone, I told Gus that I loved him. He brushed off what I said and disappeared. Yet Gus knew that he was instrumental in getting us all on the same page. This rejection of my declaration of love did not sit right with me. I went out behind the house to the large empty barn because I sensed that this is where Gus may have disappeared. I walked into the middle of the dark area and screamed at the top of my lungs—a long, long scream. Out of an immense frustration, I screamed long and loud again.

Then, from the depths of the darkness, I heard a calm voice saying, "Are you finished?" "No," I yelled back, "Who are you to decide whether I love you or not? I'm the one who told you that I love you, it's my feeling, not yours, and I know how I feel! Stop seeing things in black or white; there are many times when things are grey!" I said nothing more and he didn't answer. Nor did he come out of the shadows. I waited for what seemed to be a great length of time. I felt calm and at peace. What isn't written here is the long unspoken history that he and I share. He had received my message loud and clear: I truly did love him. We all slept in Pieter's big home that night, and I didn't see my oldest brother again before he flew back to B.C. the next morning.

When I returned home after the trip, I told Rob about my outburst and voiced my concern that my oldest brother would regret having encouraged the rest of my siblings to choose me as the spokesperson. Rob put it all into perspective and reassured me that all was well. I had not gone manic! It was obvious that I had made progress in managing my disorder.

Bonus Time

For more than a year, my father had been advised to have a T.U.R.P. (Trans Urethral Resection of the Prostate). A very dear friend of his died from the surgery, and my father sensed that his own demise would come in the same way, so he was hesitant to have the operation. He considered life after his heart attack as "bonus time," and he wanted to enjoy it. Each February, Father enjoyed a weekend celebration with his old college friends. In 1993, the gathering was in Toronto and Father asked me if I would fly with him. He had decided to attend the reunion and then let the surgeon know that he was ready to have the necessary T.U.R.P. operation.

The trip went well, and both Father and I enjoyed our time. On the flight back, Father took off his *BULOVA* watch and gave it to me very casually. I looked at him and asked, "Why are you giving this to me NOW?" He said that he no longer had need of it and wanted me to have it. This watch held a history since he had worn it every day for over a decade. His life moved forward with an acute awareness of time, and this watch had guided him for years. As much as he made little of it, I knew it was a big thing.

The Saturday after my father and I had been in Toronto, my mother phoned me early in the morning with panic and fear in her voice. In ten minutes, I was by her side. Father was not home and I found Mother in the study, slowly rocking back and forth and mumbling with a decidedly slurred speech; both hands were covering her face. "Something is wrong, something is wrong," she said. My mother's speech and facial muscles told me that she'd had a stroke. I called 911 to send an ambulance and she was admitted to the Civic Hospital. In the meantime, Father came home and I told him what had happened. My mother was admitted to a Geriatric Assessment Unit where she was a patient for the next three weeks.

Dear Treasure

Those weeks at home alone were very intense for my father. Every time I went to visit him, he was grimacing with pain while sitting in his favorite chair. I didn't need to ask, because I could tell he was having bladder spasms. I went to our doctor of almost two decades, and he prescribed Father belladonna suppositories for the pain. However, he refused to take them. Nothing was said about this because I knew that my father would appreciate the opportunity to make his own decisions. Father also knew that the frequent bladder spasms would weaken his bladder wall. I think he was pleased with my care and respect because he took to calling me "lieve schat," which means "dear treasure." As the years go by, I hold on to those two words with love, rather than feeling uncomfortable about it the way I did at the time. It wasn't like him to give endearments so frequently. I realized that he felt strongly that the surgery would be deadly.

No Stars

The evening before Father was admitted for the T.U.R.P. surgery, he visited a widow who lived in the apartment opposite his. He sang some "lustrum" (university) songs to her. The next evening I drove him to the hospital for admission. On the way to my car, he looked up at the dark sky and said," I see no stars, there are no stars." I agreed and we were on our way. During the winter there are many times when clouds high in the sky obscure the night stars. After the surgery, the surgeon gave us a report: He saw no reason why Father would not make a full recovery. However, an hour later, in a naturally lit private intensive recovery care area, I watched my father gasping for air. When he couldn't speak, the nurse quickly gave him a pen and paper and he printed, "Suffocating". He gave me one last quick panicked glance and lost consciousness.

I was asked to leave, but still saw that he was intubated and then connected to a respirator. I went to the first floor, picked up my mother (she was using a walker), and we went up the elevator to father. He was hooked up to an intravenous unit, a respirator, and some measuring units (blood pressure, blood oxygen levels), and he was in a coma. It was a short visit; she looked at him with sadness and turned, as if she couldn't bear to see him that way. As I was taking her back to her floor, she ducked into a stairwell and cried bitter tears. She hadn't looked at me the entire time that we were together. When I asked her to share with me how she was feeling, she said not a word.

When mother's medical assessments were complete, Rob and I were asked to come to the unit for a report before her discharge. At a small joint conference, we discussed what we saw as a desired plan of action for her continued care. Her medications had been adjusted and the staff had noticed that she'd had several more T.I.A.'s while in hospital (T.I.A. = Transient Ischemic Attack= small strokes). The recommendation was that she no longer live independently in her apartment. Rob and I went home and worked hard at getting our study turned into a "hospital room" for my mother. The next morning she came to live our home; it was the ninth day post surgery for father.

To and For

Father never came out of intensive care. I phoned several times a day to get a report and as the days went by, it was more and more apparent that he was in a decline from which he would not recover. Father had originally requested that "all the stops be pulled out," which meant that he wanted all efforts possible made for a continued quality of life. Every day, I kept my brothers and sisters up to date. On the eighth and ninth day, it was clear to me that the end was near, but everyone needed to be in agreement with the decisions made. Father was given more frequent and stronger electrical jolts to restart his failing heart. His kidneys had completely failed, and he was on dialysis. On the tenth day post surgery, he had another cardiac arrest and needed repeated stronger jolts before his heart weakly responded. I said to Rob," There comes a time when you are doing something TO the body instead of FOR the body." Rob understood and agreed. I updated all the brothers and sisters on father's condition. The life support systems were removed later that morning.

Inner Awareness

Without being told, my mother was aware of the changes that were happening. Her husband of over 60 years was dying, and she was listless and seemed to be in shock. The day was March 5th, 1993, and it was also my 48th birthday. Mother had little to say. At 4:30 pm in a local store, I looked at Father's watch on my wrist and "felt" his passing. At 5:00pm, when I was back at home, Rob told me that while he was taking Mother to the bathroom, she had twisted her ankle. She was uncooperative, confused, and agitated. At the same time, my sister called and said that Father had passed away at 4:30pm, just as I had felt. A nurse arrived, and we explained to my mother that she was there to help. Mother continually looked down and did not ask any questions. I was "feeling" her anger, grief, and sadness, all rolled into one. I had not told her at that time that Father had died, because in her confusion and with us leaving for my birthday dinner, I would not be there to support her reaction.

Birthday and Funeral

Rob took me out to dinner for my birthday and for a few hours we were able to decompress and talk with each other about the whirlwind of events. We shared all the emotions that we had experienced in the last few months. We were both so grateful that I had not gone manic. We agreed that the palliative care courses that I was taking were a huge support. We planned the actions that we would take in the next few days. The funeral arrangements were made and the obituary was placed in the Ottawa newspaper, as well as in a major Dutch newspaper. The visitation and funeral were held at a stately home that had been renovated into a funeral home. Emotions ran high and I was personally so grateful that I knew Clive, the funeral director, who understood that a calm empathy was just what we all needed. Mother still said very little; she used her walker for every step, and moved as if in shock.

Family Care

When my mother was discharged from the Civic Hospital, we had a social worker, Ann, who helped us with everything that was happening in our family. This lovely lady organized a family meeting where we sat in a circle in our dining room. I had honestly told Ann that I was in fear of going manic with all the stress that was placed on our core family. So, the first thing she told the children was that she was caring for the whole family by looking after me. Ann also agreed that arranging for my mother to go to a nursing home was of immediate concern. With her evident confusion and dementia, my mother would benefit from this move being done as simply as was possible. As a result, mother was transferred to "Island Lodge" within the week. She went to her empty apartment one last time before she went to the Lodge. During that visit she sat on her walker seat, looked around at the empty living room, and said nothing.

The only time I let my tears flow was while I was taking my morning showers. The hot water seemed to set me off. Our children were great—very sympathetic and loving. Rob and I were aware that we had lost both my father and my mother in quick succession. The first time Mary and I visited mother days later at "Island Lodge," she was smiling and moving faster with her walker. We had a walk together outside on the grounds and then a cup of tea in the coffee shop, and she even talked a bit! I had high hopes that we had turned a corner.

Miracles

Before her strokes started, mother used to like reading magazines about Herbert W. Armstrong. He founded "The Philadelphia Church of God," and small monthly publications were made by his organization, which still provides publications on request today. Mr. Armstrong wrote the book, *The Incredible Human Potential*, in which he describes God's plan for us, His children. The book was first printed in 1978. During this tumultuous period of my life, I read that book again, and I loved it. It helps confirm that there is no such thing as coincidence. For the three years that Mother was at "Island Lodge," I had only one patient that I looked after for five days a week. This patient was just a few blocks away from where Mother was living. Both my patient and my mother died within weeks of each other. If you look for them, you will find the miracles that are evident within your life.

The 5 Ps

Even though these years were hard, I was able to keep my depression at bay. It was during this period that I identified some key tactics to staying positive and healthy.

Here are the Five P's that will help rid you of depression:

1. *Potential*
2. *Participation*
3. *Peace*
4. *Power*
5. *Passion*

To reach our Potential we need to Participate. In doing so, we will achieve Peace, thereby giving us control over our lives. The sense of purpose that we gain with greater control will give us a sense of Power and continued Peace, which will help us avoid feeling frustrated. In addition, we will increase our Passion rather than our apathy, which can only abound when all hope is lost. Put these 5 P's together and a sense of *purpose* is the result. Having a purpose is why we are alive, so these 5 P's are truly the key to *living* our best lives.

Curtain Calls:

- *Respect your elders. Step up when the time comes to take an active role in caring for them. Look at the 5 P's: Stepping up is participation in its best form.*
- *Share your love with family. When all else fails, your family is meant for support.*
- *Many are not interested in anything religious. Do not impose your own beliefs and avoid judging others.*
- *Apathy is to be avoided at all costs. There is a great variety of subjects that may genuinely pique your interest—take the time to find what excites you.*
- *Nurture a love of reading. This will help you stay away from addictive, time-wasting behavior.*
- *Give yourself plenty of abundance in generosity of time, good feelings, and money—this means sharing your abundance with those you love.*

CHAPTER 13

Moving On...

When Paul was a baby, Rob and I were told that he would be no taller than five feet maximum, if he survived. This prophecy was imbedded in my brain, and was so painful to comprehend: our child, destined to live with an uncertain and difficult future. I prayed and cried and prayed and cried that he would grow up to be healthy and happy. As parents, Rob and I did our best. Many, many prayers have been answered and I am so very grateful. Today, all three of our children are tall, above average in height. The lesson that I learned from this is that hope is given through prayer, and prayer is real. With prayer, I was able to give my grief over to the Trinity and accept any situation or outcome with true gratitude. I am so grateful for Rob and our three children, their spouses, and our grandchildren.

Donor Match

When Paul finished high school, it seemed that he ran out of energy. The numbers for his kidney function were getting worse. We had not allowed him to participate in any contact sports, and so he found a non-contact sport, curling, that he still enjoys playing competitively to this day. Rob, Peter and I were tested for being a donor kidney match for Paul. I wouldn't let Mary be tested because I didn't want her to be in the compromising position of saying no if she was a match. Of the three of us, I was the best match. I was thrilled for the solution we had found, and was ever so glad that Paul was going to receive my kidney! On November 24th, 1995, Paul and I were in adjoined operating rooms, each with our own team of surgeons and support staff. Paul had an A- blood type and mine was O+. I asked his surgeon how it was that Paul could receive my kidney, and he explained that as much blood as possible was gently squeezed out before giving it to Paul. The Rhesus factor was no issue. Also, to facilitate the removal, the surgeon took out my lower rib. Our recoveries were good and nineteen years later we're both enjoying quality lives. Praise modern science! Paul is now well educated with a lovely wife and son, so again I say, prayers can be answered.

Peaceful Sunset

In March of 1996, Rob and I were called to his parents' home. His mom had just had a massive brain aneurism that sent her to the Civic Hospital for a nine-hour surgery. For an 82 year old, this length of time under an anesthetic is devastating; however, she survived. She was admitted to a long-term care facility where her nurses were attentive and well qualified. We all visited often. Once, she came home to her own back yard for an afternoon in the mid-summer, but she looked physically and mentally overwhelmed from all the effort. On Sept. 26th, 1996, we were all called to her bedside because she was breathing her last. In the late afternoon, Rob went to the end of the hall of her floor and was comforted by the most beautiful sunset that he had ever seen. Within that hour, she died peacefully.

Farewell

In the three years that my mother was at Island Lodge, I visited her once or twice every week. Her decline was slow and we were told that only an autopsy would determine if she had dementia or Alzheimer's disease. She died on Nov. 6th, 1996. The staff phoned me that day so that I could arrive on time to say good-bye. Because she had been "gone" spiritually many months earlier, her death was less painful for me. In my heart, I had already bid her farewell.

Family Gifts

In the summer of 1997, all of my five siblings who were still alive spent two weeks with our oldest brother, Gus, in British Columbia. Gus, who had been a passionate high school English teacher, gave us the present of watching a new BBC series called "Pride and Prejudice." Gus's gift was the interpretation and explanation of this Jane Austen novel turned television show. He wanted to have us all together because he had cancer and knew that his time was limited. We all bonded and it was a wonderful family gathering. A year later, our oldest brother was gone.

Millennium Changes

Our daughter Mary was married in 1999, and the wedding was a happy and beautiful celebration of love. After the millennium change, I struggled more and more with suicidal thinking. In 2001, I had another manic episode just when I thought they would no longer happen. As usual, I made my grandiose declaration of being Jesus. I knew what I was doing. It wasn't apathy that did me in; it was my passion. With my manic episode came physical setbacks as well, due to injuring my knee in a bad fall. The injury wasn't healing, so I stopped working in 2001. A year later

I fell more often, hurting both knees, and I considered myself at a high risk for injury. My nephrectomy (kidney removal) gave me a flank hernia that was thankfully repaired.

During this time, I was uncontrollably gaining weight. The Weight Management Clinic at the Ottawa Civic Hospital helped both Mary and myself. However, the weight program that worked for Mary didn't work as well for me, so it was advised that I undergo a gastric bypass. Because the wait in Toronto was too long, the provincial health care system paid for my surgery to take place in New York in October of 2004. I was 286 lbs. and considered morbidly obese. After the surgery, I lost eighty pounds and then hit a wall; however, I was satisfied with the changes I was able to make.

Rob's dad moved to a retirement home in 2002 and in the summer of 2003, started a decline from which he didn't recover. He was the same as my mother—confused and unaware of his environment. He went to a long-term care facility and six months later, he was gone. It was March of 2004.

Exit Left

My urge to commit suicide became stronger. My back pain was chronic despite the fact that I had an excellent chiropractor. He was adjusting me with a lot of force twice a month just to keep me going. Every day, I drove Rob to his work downtown and picked him up again so that I could keep the car for all my appointments. These trips took forty minutes or so each time, thirty of which were on the highway. Each day I wanted to "exit right" off the highway, in other words, I wanted to die. If I gave the steering wheel a sudden pull with my right arm, it would be done. I looked for places with a cement post or bridge so that I would be dead, not just severely injured. I denied myself the urge every time, and vowed to only "exit left," meaning I vowed to keep on living.

The years from 2000 to 2007 turned out to be some of my most dangerous years. I underwent daily struggles that I shared with no one. I didn't fear suicide, but I knew that it was not God's plan for me. Each day, I did not give in, even though it was a daily struggle with no known beginning and no known end. These struggles taught me two important "myths" about suicide: Not every suicidal person wants to hurt others in the process, and not every suicidal person shares their struggle. This is because writing or talking about suicide puts it out into the universe and gives it power. When the struggle is already intense, a single thought can kill you.

Travel and Respite

Rob worked at Natural Resources Canada, and in 2003 he was asked to be the Chairman of the Working Group on Statistics in The Kimberley Process. His job involved issuing government certificates that were given to reduce the "blood diamonds" in circulation worldwide. The movie *Blood Diamond* depicts the culture well. Rob's job allowed us to travel frequently, and each time we visited other parts of the world, there was a break in my suicidal thinking. I was grateful for the respite, every time.

Oom Cees

On May 5th, 2004, Oom Cees died. We had already booked a trip to Holland for June and couldn't change it, so it took us a month to get to Tante Jannie. On June 5th, 2004, Oom Cees's brother died; we were able to attend his funeral. I deeply felt Tante Jannie's grief and didn't understand why it was potentiating mine. How was it possible for me to feel so much grief? I know that Tante Jannie received our love and comfort in sharing Oom Cees's loss. She was stunned, and at 85 she felt lonely in every fiber of her being. She told me that being old made it harder for her to bear. But she was determined to stay put in the home that had been built by the Royal Family to house them in their retirement. The home mirrored "The Aardhuis" of my younger years. I apologized to Tante Jannie for not being with her a month earlier. Her forgiveness was in her eyes. Oom Cees's cremated ashes were in an urn that Tante Jannie kept on a shelf in her bedroom.

Precious Visits

From 2004 until November 2011 when she died, T.J. lived independently in her home. During those years, Rob and I had the good fortune to be able to visit her twice a year, every year. Those visits were so precious. She was really pleased that Rob liked to visit, and I told Rob many times how much we appreciated his love and patience—he smiled and understood every time. Tante Jannie had regular visits from a number of friends and relatives who all let her know how much they loved her. She was at the point where she was receiving what she had been giving all her life: love was her harvest and the harvest was priceless. Some people call it karma and some people say, "What goes around, comes around."

After each precious visit, Rob and I would leave with the thought that "this" would be the last time we saw her alive. But then six months later she was there for us to visit again. In the summer of 2006, she told me about the shaft of light that shone once through the trees on her daily walk. She showed me the exact spot and she said that she knew it was Oom Cees in spirit form. He was telling her that he was all right, and that he was waiting for her.

God answers prayers; I'm convinced of it. But there are many prayers that I have that don't get answered, which just reinforces that He is in charge. He answered my prayer of asking for good care for Tante Jannie. For as long as I could remember, she loved to smoke a cigarette every now and then. The doctor told her that the little smoking she enjoyed would make no significant difference. She loved it when I sat with her and watched her enjoy a cigarette without judgment.

Show of Recognition

In mid-April of 1996, my oldest sister, Agatha, died suddenly from a deep vein thrombosis. She collapsed while in the hospital and nothing could be done to save her. Most of her siblings and all of her children were at the funeral that was held in New Brunswick where she lived. My brother Pieter, my other sister and I, all drove together for this sad event. I was overwhelmed with surprise and pride as I watched the funeral procession move by with a police and military honor escort. Pieter explained that Agatha had been writing an account of the feelings of the Canadian soldiers who liberated the Dutch people. She wrote about the deep and abiding love and respect that the Dutch have for their Canadian liberators. This was her Master's degree research, and since the authorities were aware of her project, they gave a show of recognition and respect.

Gone!

From November 2006 to November 2007, I needed the use of a walker to move about. My chronic pain was intolerable and I leaned heavily on the walker to take the weight off my painful lower back. On a pain scale from 1 (low) to 10 (high), I was usually at an 8 or 9. I was referred to a chronic pain clinic in Ottawa to investigate whether the cause of my pain was related to arthritis or cancer. The orthopedic surgeon determined that there was no role for back surgery; however, I had a gut feeling that only back surgery would give me relief, and I was right. Rob and I saw a news story on a Canadian man who had successful spinal surgery in Chennai, India. Upon doing some research, we discovered an option closer to home—the Laser Spine Institute in Tampa, Florida. My doctors in Ottawa disagreed with our decision to go, but we booked the flight anyway. I had the minimally invasive surgery, got off the operating table, and with my walker made it back to our hotel room, 200 or 300 yards away. The inflamed, irritated L5S1 nerve was released during the surgery and my chronic pain was gone! All that was left was a bit of surgical pain. The next day I said to Rob, "My suicidal thinking is gone!" Amazing. It's been gone ever since!

In November 2008, Rob was gone to India for work on *The Kimberley Process*. I hadn't wanted to expose myself to seeing the widespread poverty in the country, so I stayed at home. While he was gone, I woke up early and went to a restaurant alone every morning. Before I knew it, I had gone manic again. And just as before, my belief that I was the reincarnated Jesus Christ was met with a negative reaction. When was I going to absorb this lesson so that I wouldn't continue to be embarrassed and ashamed? After all this time, I could read a judgment made even when a person's facial muscles were kept carefully neutral. Three friends of mine came to visit and I couldn't help but share my joy of knowing that I was the Chosen One. With sympathy they explained that this was not possible. It was easy for me to read the horror on their faces. They've since forgiven me for making such a bold declaration. My sister came with a gift (a soft well-made beige blanket) that lifted my heart. Rob returned just before I was discharged and visited me with a sadness in his eyes that I had hoped to never see again.

Determination

Determined to follow the practices that would strengthen my mind, I took an Advanced Usui Tibetan Reiki course from Jacqueline Fairbrass in January of 2009. We downloaded so much energy that I was amazed.

From that day on, I meditated every day for an hour or more every time. I could "feel" the meditations helping. I started thinking more about my religious beliefs and why I thought the way I did. I read the *Bible* daily, but I didn't share this with others because discussing religious points of view just wasn't safe for me. My faith grew and I started to feel a joy that I never thought possible.

For about ten years I committed myself to "Exit Left" (on the road) so that I wouldn't commit suicide. I endured a daily mental fight to stay alive; thankfully, my suicidal thinking disappeared and now I am alive and able to write this book. I hope that my struggle and survival can be of service to you. Truly, if I can overcome, so can you. I do indeed have my life back. Hallelujah! And I can talk about my religious feelings without going manic. Hallelujah again! I have no idea what God has planned for me, but let me reassure you that my bi-polar disorder is history. I truly desire that you too will overcome any illness, disorder, or unhealthy mental state, and reclaim your life.

Curtain Calls:

- *You may be able to lessen suicidal thinking by changing your routine, or eliminating chronic pain.*
- *Without talking about suicide, which may be dangerous for you, seek comfort and love from those you can trust.*
- *People behind the phones at Crisis Centers are trained to talk you past your panic moments.*
- *Recognizing and accepting your feelings, is the first step to recovery.*
- *Foster forgiveness within yourself. Forgive yourself as well as the person who needs your forgiveness. When we do not forgive, we poison our own spirit.*
- *Meditation is now a recognized method to calm a troubled mind. Start meditating 5 minutes a day, and you will see results.*

- *Practice makes perfect! This especially refers to meditating.*
- *Prayer is real, and it works. But don't expect all your prayers to be answered. Trust that the Universe is unfolding as it should.*

CHAPTER 14

A Healthy Mind: Never Looking Back

In January of 2012, I made the conscious decision to give all my cares to the Lord. This was done with the intent of progressing further along my journey towards mental and spiritual health. In the process of my personal growth, it was the best decision for my life, but I am not suggesting that you need to do the same. We are each the sum total of all the experiences and people who come into our lives. The gift of choosing our own path, our own journey, is a gift that I hold dear. Non-judgment is an important part of this privilege. I would love to see all societies become non-judgmental. This can happen if we take a responsibility to follow the commandments that are basic for all of us.

For example, the Ten Commandments are basic for all of us. Read them carefully and then focus on following these Commandments. One of them is: " Thou shalt not kill." Giving in to suicide is murdering yourself. God loves you and when you meditate, you will start "feeling" His love. If it works for me, then it will work for you because God is no respecter of persons. Practice meditating. It works. If someone you love committed suicide, know that God would have forgiven him. It is for you to forgive as well.

My decision to trust *fully* in the Lord coincided with my discontinuation of antipsychotics,which in turn released my imaginative thinking. I am so grateful that my clarity of mind is improving as the months and years go by. The fear of going manic is gone. After dealing with over ten manic episodes, and countless "amber states," I wanted no more. My daily meditations and *Bible* readings help me a great deal. You have the freedom of choice to discover the methods of healing that work best for you. You don't have to do the same thing that I did to succeed, but you do have to *want* to enjoy better health.

Priorities

After Rob retired in early 2009, we were both able to focus on our priorities. We sold our home of 35 years and downsized to a house where our bedroom is on the ground floor. Rob and I both love our new home. For many years our youngest child, Mary, had asked us to demolish the family cottage and build an all-season home on the same property. The cottage, built by Rob's family, held a lot of family history and I worried that it would be disrespectful to their memories to demolish what they had built. However, Dr. Molot taught us about the accumulative damages of breathing in an environment that was built with toxic materials, which were standard in the 1960's when the cottage was erected. Based upon this knowledge, Rob and I made the decision to move forward with Mary's dream.

Peter, Mary, Rob and myself, worked on the design of the new home together. The four of us all contributed significantly to the final result. Our son Paul was not involved because he and his family were living in another country. (We miss him, but we're in touch every week). Neighbors on the same lake, just a few properties away, had very kindly let us see their new cottage for inspiration. Our plans were voted on and accepted by the township council, and we began construction in the fall of 2010. We still call it the "cottage," even though it is our permanent home in the country.

Tante Jannie

In June of 2011, Rob and I visited Tante Jannie and found out that she'd had a brief stay in a nursing home. She was so fiercely independent that she managed to get herself home again with the help her niece! I asked, but T.J. wouldn't let me stay with her to give her my care; she said that Rob needed me. For the past several decades she had also requested that I phone her no more than once a week, and I did what I was told. It hurt that my involvement was limited, but there was no maliciousness with her rejection; she said "no" out of love. She reminded me again that once she was in spirit form, she would "talk to me" from a cloud, and we both found pleasure in the prospect.

On the morning of November 1st, 2011, my cousin, Minie (Tante Jannie's niece), phoned and said that T.J. was close to taking her last breath. She had pneumonia and was not recovering. Minie phoned a few hours later and told us that she had died peacefully. Minie said that her last words in Dutch, translated into English, were: "Now I have to wait until June", (June was the month of Rob's and my visits). Within hours, I flew to Holland. Rob organized things at home and joined me two days later. We were given the pleasure of staying with my youngest brother, Oncko and his wife for the duration of our stay in Holland. Coming home to my brother's place after emotional days was a huge comfort, and I felt very grateful to Oncko and my sister-law for this relief.

Tante Jannie was lying in an open coffin in a small room at the funeral home in Apeldoorn. There was a straight chair on each side of her and many flower arrangements on the floor. The room smelled heavenly. I looked at her and had the urge to hug her, even though I knew that her spirit was elsewhere in the room, not in her body. I was alone, and I put my hands on her upper arms and very gently brushed her cheek with mine. I didn't cry; instead, I felt at peace. Tante Jannie had expressed the desire to be with Oom Cees so many times, and finally she was with him—she got her wish. I could feel her calm spirit in the room and it comforted me.

Rob made it on time for the cremation service. There were hundreds of family members and friends at the service. I was very grateful that I was able to give one of the eulogies; it was well received. I "felt" the celebration of her life, which is exactly why we were there. I spoke of her love for the many people who crossed her path, and I gave thanks that I was fortunate enough to be one of them. The sense of closure for me on that day was tremendous. My cousin Minie, who has T.J.'s wedding ring, gave me Oom Cees' wedding ring. The cross necklace that I wear every day has Oom Cees' ring on it—it sits close to my heart.

Reiki Master

Back in Canada, Wendy, the receptionist for my chiropractor, offered to teach me the Reiki Master course in January of 2012. This was a daylong one-on-one course between Wendy and myself. After completing the course, I could tell that my meditations were even more effective. Wendy also teaches I.E.T. (Integrated Energy Therapy), which is incorporated into her Reiki treatment. For many months, Wendy gave me monthly Reiki treatments. The healing energy that these visits gave me was priceless.

Stability

For the last few years I have had a very good psychiatrist. My appointments were every three weeks, and Rob was invited to join me anytime. Rob came to an appointment in January of 2012 when I asked for permission to discontinue the daily antipsychotics; Rob promised to monitor me closely. The psychiatrist approved, and on January 31st, 2012 these drugs were deleted from my daily regime. After several more visits, Rob came with me again and we asked if I could have an appointment every three months rather than every three weeks. Mentally, I was feeling very stable. It had been four years since I'd had a suicidal thought. I was sleeping well and feeling healthy. My anniversary of being antipsychotic free is celebrated every year. My visits to the psychiatrist are now semi-annual.

Feeling Spirits

I take immense pleasure in feeling the spirit of Tante Jannie around me. She is not on a cloud far away, but rather she is right next to me. I feel her more than I have ever felt my parents, Oom Cees, my oldest sister, or brother. I am amazed at the great comfort this has given me, and I have discovered that there are many others who share the same experience of "feeling spirits." Rob has told me that he does not feel his parents, but that doesn't stop him from visiting their gravesites every week and hauling up different memories every time he goes. Rob accepts that my feelings are real and that there is no right or wrong answer: We are allowed to be who we are.

Coming Home

In March of 2012, I was at the Weight Management Clinic for an annual visit when another patient in the room looked at me and said, "Oh, what an ugly hat you're wearing!" That was the beginning of Wendy B. and I becoming friends. She is one of the most generous people that I have ever met! A few months later, Wendy B. told me about a friend she worked with who had invited her to a women's prayer group. There was no hesitation for me—I asked if I could come and Wendy said "yes!" When Wendy and I both started going to the bi- monthly morning-prayer group, I felt like I had come home. The love and energy that I felt in the room has inspired me to recommend it to everyone who feels lonely, or who feels like "something is missing." The "it" that I am referring to is finding and joining a group that celebrates love, joy and peace. Our prayer group praises the Lord, Jesus, and for the few hours that we are together, our common bond is the love and faith that we feel for God. We all recognize the Holy Spirit that we feel and the strong sense of like-minded community that gives us a very strong sense of peace, joy and love from within. The faith and healing that I feel for myself is awesomely liberating for me and I want to work to give you what I have found.

Super Foods

Wendy L., my Reiki Master, released forty pounds and I was impressed. I asked her what she had done and she told me about the super food products. A whole new World opened up for me when I started eating these foods. I lost 19 pounds in my first month! This isn't just a food product—it is a life style change that encourages you to step out of your comfort zone. Within the program I have found a culture of family and have received free personal growth coaching. The results are real!

My coach, Cindy Little, invited me to a monthly speaker's training session called "Your Stage" hosted by Steve Lowell in Ottawa. He was so good the first time I saw him that I thought he was a professional from a much larger city than Ottawa. He is an excellent coach for teaching someone how to be effective on stage. Speaking in public is his expertise and I pray that he coaches me. Years earlier, I had read "The Secret", "The Power" and "The Magic" by Rhonda Byrne. I wanted to experience that for real; I believed it was possible. With these foods, suddenly I was experiencing it and living it everyday! Within a few months, I had released fifty pounds and fit into a size 12 pants! That hadn't happened since I was a teenager!

These food products gave me a change in lifestyle that I still enjoy today, and I am not planning to ever be without these foods. My mind and body love them. It has been almost three years since I've eaten any significant amount of meat, which means that I am a vegetarian. Yet, I am getting more daily protein than I've ever had in the past, and I feel great! Also, it gives me a passive income and I am glad to freely coach anyone who chooses me as mentor.

Spread the Love

In the spring of 2014, Peggy McColl was a speaker at "Your Stage", and just like that day when there was no hesitation with Wendy's invitation to the prayer group, there was no hesitation with putting myself into the light of Peggy's energy. The reason why she is so successful is that she exudes peace, joy and love. At the same time, she shares a generosity that blows my mind. She has been a personal mentor ever since, and I am very grateful and happy for her light in my life. With her guidance, I am feeling calm, at peace, joyful, and successful. I am also feeling purposeful, loving, and bold. I want to share these feelings with you: I want to show you my peace. Rob and I both now have a sense of purpose that was unimaginable just three years ago. My goal now is to motivate and inspire a new generation of people who are feeling stressed, suicidal, lost, hopeless, and alone. I want to share with you a way to overcome grief. I am not a mental health professional; I am an elder with experience.

Pieter Trip

My brother, Pieter, lives just an hour's drive from us. The close proximity allows us to see each other easily and often over the years and we have benefitted greatly from each other and our families. In 2009, after years of giving freely of his knowledge concerning trees, he wrote a book about them. Rob and I are so happy and grateful that our nutritional lifestyle has improved our physical and financial health. Pieter discovered that essential minerals given to trees improve their health and longevity as well. Micronutrients make a huge difference! The name of Pieter's book is "Growing Great Trees". It's a practical guide to growing big, healthy trees. His love of trees shines through in this little book. His legacy is a forest at the back of his farm where he has practiced what he preaches.

Pay it Forward

In June of 2014, Penny Lee Prevost was at Steve Lowell's speaker training event and she asked me whether I would be interested in "paying it forward". I said, "yes" and she explained to me what the movement of "The Graduit" is all about. I am now a happy member of this organization. Opportunities like this continue to come into my life, and I know there are more in the future. I want to "pay it forward." Being a part of "the Graduit" organization is a part of my plan.

For decades I have thought that I wanted my story to be in a book someday. Shortly after meeting me, Peggy invited me to her home on April 18, 2014. This was a gathering of authors and aspiring authors from all over North America. I was hooked! Peggy shared that her expertise is in teaching authors how to become successful. Her teaching is rooted in being of service to others and giving a good value. Peggy's generosity is at a level that I aspire to. I want to be of service to you and help you get past suicidal thinking and mental instability.

Now that you have read my story in *Exit Stage Left*, you've read how I rose above my adversity. I have trained my mind, and so can you. Writing my story down on paper was clarifying and cathartic. However, in publicizing my thoughts and opening up my life, I know I must be open to criticism. In today's world, it's unavoidable, but I believe we must ultimately strive to be non-judgmental. Start practicing non-judgment in your life, and you will already be on the path to peace and prosperity. With that in mind, we can all support those that live in a state of depression and sadness. That support will help to understand the disease, and through constant effort and determination, save the lives of thousands afflicted with this terrible illness.

Curtain Calls:

- *Relationships are built over time, and are based on trust, attraction, and reliability.*
- *Generosity is at the core of good values.*
- *Be authentic and honest in every aspect of your life.*
- *Even when time is short, an informed decision is still best.*
- *Foster your own physical and mental health so that you can share your improvements with others.*

ACKNOWLEDGEMENTS

Those from whom I benefitted are many. There would be pages full of names and still I would be concerned that I had missed someone important.

I thank you all from the bottom of my heart and I love you.

YOU KNOW WHO YOU ARE!!!

XOXOXOXOXOXOXO

TILLY.

EPILOGUE

Exit Stage Left
6.22.22.

When this book didn't send me into a manic episode, I felt safe. When I could tell my story and these books didn't fly off the shelf, I felt even safer.

Ideas come to creative people like me. Suddenly, I knew that an exit had and an entrance as well. Right is the opposite of left. I had the title of my next book,

Enter Stage Right

Because I was able to share my story in a shallow manner, I felt confident. I love writing, and I know that now. With this next book, I will share more of my thoughts. My in-depth shares are meant to help you.

Xoxox

Love, Tilly.